I thoroughly enjoyed reading the chapters. Elizabeth Ralston has the ability to write and to write well, with purpose and with passion. She has shown us how the society that we have been brought up in has dictated many of the values that we are supposed to be acclimated to; and when we challenged them, we are like a 'fish swimming upstream'. I hope that her book's message gets to the 'masses' and that it can reach many others who can identify with its message and meaning.

— Jean S.
Member, 12-Step Recovery Program

As a recovering codependent for many years, I have often asked myself: where does my codependency come from? This book answers part of that question for me, by linking the training that girls receive in femininity with adult codependent thoughts and actions. It is written in a clear and intelligent manner, with many references to classic literature in the field.

— Liz H.
Member, 12-Step Recovery Program

The Mother and the Manager is a thinking person's book for anyone, especially one recovering from codependency. Elizabeth weaves research with personal insights that shed light on one's own personal history. She is definitely informing my own recovery path.

—Grace M.
Member, 12-Step Recovery Program

The Mother and the Manager has helped me gain perspective in how our cultural roles have created barriers toward our developing healthy relationships, and how this process has affected all of us. This book has helped me develop more patience and understanding in my relationships with others. I'm very grateful for its hopeful message.

—Sarah A.
Member, 12-Step Recovery Program

The Mother
And The Manager

*Uncovering the Codependent Nature of
Our Male and Female Cultural Roles*

Elizabeth Ralston

ISBN: 978-1-962363-10-5 (sc)
ISBN: 978-1-962363-11-2 (hc)
ISBN: 978-1-962363-12-9 (e)

Rev. date: 10/11/2023

For all of those in my circle of family and friends
who have intentionally engaged in relationships with
those they care about, based on the goals of equality
and partnership and guided by the ideals of love,
understanding and mutual commitment.

Contents

Acknowledgements

A number of people lent me invaluable support in writing this book, by either giving me information, feedback, encouragement, or all three. I'd first like to express my gratitude to Dr. Riane Eisler and Dr. Allan G. Johnson, both of whom encouraged me in this project. Receiving support from these two well-known and established authors was extremely important to me, especially since I used so many of their concepts in my work. Their insights and conclusions were invaluable in helping me formulate my own arguments towards an ethic of partnership and equality between men and women. I'd also like to express my thanks to the eight individuals, four men and four women, all of whom had been involved in twelve-step recovery programs, who contributed to this book by anonymously sharing their stories of recovery which helped to illustrate different patterns of codependency and which are found in the fourth chapter of my book. Several individuals took the time to review various chapters of my book and give me their feedback. These are Dr. Jody Kolodzey, Elizabeth Heller, Kathie Murphy, Jenny Rolufs, Toni Zuper, Christa Fabiani, Jean Steinmetz, Amy Trust, Alisa Oswalt, Denise Saltz Bunker, Reverend Addae Ama Kraba and my sister, Marjorie Ralston Taggart. My husband Stephen Nasobkow, has been consistently unwavering in his encouragement and moral support throughout the lengthy process of research and writing.

Five mental health professionals reviewed various parts of my work and gave me important feedback. I wish to thank Ms. Ginger Edwards and Ms. Elizabeth Kuptferman, both licensed professional counselors who specialize in codependency, as well as professional psychotherapists Mr. Kenneth Renn, Dr. Mona Cardell, and Dr. Laura Windham.

Lastly, I'd like to express my profound gratitude to Dr. Maryanne T. Romano, professional psychotherapist. Dr. Romano was associated with me from the beginning of this project and consistently gave me encouragement and support throughout its odyssey. It was clear to me from the beginning, as it is today, that the support I received from Dr. Romano was directly related to my being able to research, write and complete this book. I remain deeply indebted to her for being my mentor and advocate throughout this very important work.

Introduction

Most people who are codependent are more concerned with the health and well-being of others than they are with their own lives. They suffer from low self esteem, an inability to set boundaries and an obsessive need to control others, either directly or indirectly. After attending meetings of Co-dependents Anonymous for less than a year, I sensed that something essential was missing for me in my attempts to deal with my own codependent behaviors through this program. Although the official position of Co-dependents Anonymous is that codependent behaviors are rooted primarily in the dysfunctional home, intuitively I sensed that, at least for me, this statement was only partially true.

Intense and vivid memories added to my feelings of discomfort, memories of having been raised as a girl in the 1950's and 1960's, where traditional gender roles were considered the norm. Their strength was reinforced by recollections of other women I knew in the program who shared similar experiences from their childhoods and periods of adolescence with me. All of our memories had similar themes. As young women we were most often asked to forfeit our personal dreams and ambitions in order to marry and become mothers and homemakers. Rather than finding and expressing our true selves, we were asked to adopt pleasing and compliant personas. Instead of learning to think and speak for ourselves, we were taught to be "good girls" who were overly concerned with pleasing others, not making mistakes, and being "nice" to everyone.

In her book, *The Curse of the Good Girl,* Rachel Simmons compares the "good" girl with the "real" girl, who stays connected to a strong inner core of her thoughts, feelings and desires. Simmons adds that, in contrast to the good girl, the real girl is able not only to listen to who she is, but also to act on this knowledge.[1] Through our "good girl" personas each of us was forced to play the role of a traditional woman, which was, at its very core, codependent. As a codependent, the traditional woman learns to control indirectly, most often by being "nice" and by "people pleasing."

In comparison to women, men have been taught to play a traditional male role that has asked them to adhere to a "male" code which severely restricts their ability to feel, respond and experience life authentically. Although the behaviors that men are asked to adopt to be considered masculine are not as traditionally codependent as are those of women, men exhibit codependent behaviors when they are asked to consider the evaluations and judgments of other men before they feel that they have "made it" as men. In addition, men demonstrate codependency when they define their sense of what it is to be a man by how well they can dominate and control women and other men. In doing so, they can severely restrict their emotional lives. In his book *The Flying Boy,* John Lee describes his intense need to maintain control:

Control. I couldn't let go because I had to be in control of my emotions. I had to be in control of my world, and, whenever possible, other people's worlds as well. I had to control Laural through manipulation, education and domination, while paying lip service to feminism and equality. I always had to be in control. I could never be late. I couldn't stand to be kept waiting – control in a hundred different ways. If I could just control or maintain the illusion of control by predicting and programming my existence and environment, I thought I might just have a chance in this world.[2]

While growing up I had often observed the men in my family demonstrate this obsessive need to control. They would lecture, rather than discuss, issue an order rather than make a request, maintain a mistaken opinion, rather than admit to an error. Their behaviors would reinforce my own traditional "feminine" behaviors: in response to their lectures and orders I would listen rather than speak, accept rather than question, obey rather than speak up. By responding to their dominance with my passivity, I was unwittingly giving them permission to exert control over me. From having my door held at a restaurant to having the bill "taken care of" by a male companion, I was mired in gender-based co-dependent behaviors, which, by their very nature, reinforced the behaviors I was seeking to eliminate in my recovery program. Repeated over and over again, these stereotyped behaviors created an entrenched and circular pattern between myself and my male counterparts, eliciting widely divergent "passive" and "dominant" styles of relating between us, styles which contributed more to withdrawal, mistrust and unhealthy interactions, than to mutuality, trust and effective communication.

Although as men and women we are conditioned to exhibit typically "male" or "female" behaviors, most of our day-to-day behaviors are a combination of both. Men can, at times, be passive and compliant. Conversely, women, especially those who work in employment settings, can learn to be quite effective at managing others. We can be subordinate in some areas of our lives, while playing a more dominant role in others. The predicament is not as simple as a conflict between two individuals, where one seeks to dominate another; the core of the dilemma occurs when one group's domination over another is culturally sanctioned, supported by our institutions, and is therefore accepted as "normal." At some point in my research for this book, I began to realize that the true culprit, if there was one, was our patriarchal society, which has encouraged us to behave in only a narrowly approved range considered appropriate for our respective genders.

Since the 1980's, however, rapid changes in the economic structure in the United States, where large numbers of blue-collar manufacturing jobs, traditionally occupied by men, were lost or outsourced and were accompanied by a commensurate increase of lower paying service jobs, created an environment where women, for the first time in history, could enter the work force in large numbers. Although previously men's status as men depended on their ability to perform the bread-winning role as heads of households, now, they had to share this role with women, most of whom proved capable of holding and sustaining full time employment, even while they maintained their jobs as mothers and homemakers. This pattern has continued unabated into the present time, where women now make up fifty percent of the work force; it has contributed to a transformation in the traditional roles that men and women now play in relationship to one another, a change of monumental proportions. Yet, without much fanfare, this conversion has taken place very rapidly, within the span of only fifty years.

Such rapid-fire changes over such a short period of time have left many of us catching our breaths. For some of us, these changes have created the need to drastically evaluate our early conditioning and how it has impacted us into the present time. Although my efforts to reclaim my personal history specifically relating to my gender conditioning has contributed, to a large degree, to real progress in my recovery from codependency, I was amazed by the utter failure of most authors to mention the role culture and gender roles have played in the development of codependency in most of the recovery literature that I read.

I suspected that most women's experiences with the twelve-step recovery group of Co-Dependents Anonymous were similar to mine. And yet, because any mention of gender conditioning was, to a large degree, lacking in the recovery literature, few of these women had any guidance to know how to deal effectively with their gender issues within the context of this program. I would observe women coming in and out of the recovery rooms, hesitant and unsure. It was as if they questioned if they even had a right to be there, and remain "good" wives, mothers or daughters.

I've written this book for women who, like me, were raised to be codependent by virtue of their gender role, a role that, although it was taught to us by our parents, was nevertheless reinforced by other powerful forces in our society, such as our religions, educational institutions and work places. Many of these women would come to meetings and leave feeling overwhelmed or confused by culturally prescribed roles which appeared to be in direct contradiction to what are considered "healthy" recovery behaviors. The effort to change these roles was most likely overwhelming for them, just as it was for me when I first began my recovery program.

I've also written this book for men. Over the years I've observed men who seemed inhibited about sharing their experiences in meetings; I suspect that this pattern may have been caused, in part, because their conditioning as men prohibited them from exposing their inner thoughts and feelings to others. I'm certain there were many others who never made it to meetings, as admitting that they might have a problem might make them appear less manly, or "in control" of themselves and/or their emotions. In addition, the injunctions widely followed by men which encourage them to repress feelings such as anger, grief or sadness can contribute to a wide variety of addictions, enabling them to mask, rather than to confront, their hidden feelings. Finally, adherence to the "male code" often causes men to experience their feelings such as fear or anxiety with shame, rather than enabling them to accept these feelings as a normal part of the human experience.

Finally, men and women forced to relate to each other only through the lenses of gender are neither able to completely affirm their own humanity, nor the humanity of the other. Men conditioned to dominate often learn to treat women as subordinate "others," who exist primarily to service their needs. Women, conditioned to be subordinates, often resort to passive and indirect manipulation of men in order to fulfill their needs. In doing so, they fail to develop the skills necessary to foster the independence, self-esteem and confidence necessary for survival in today's society. Restricted by gender stereotypes, such individuals never develop the sense of "wholeness" necessary to participate in truly equal relationships based on cooperation and collaboration, where each partner is given the opportunity to experience his or her true potential as a human being.

I welcome all individuals who read this book to join me in examining these gender-based patterns within the historical context of the patriarchal structure that we, as a society, have inherited. Created by societies to enable them to survive in earlier times, our social institutions cannot exist without our collective permission. Although we may continue to find aspects of our current system to be helpful and necessary for our individual and collective survival, it's becoming increasingly obvious that it contains unhealthy, negative attributes that are unsupportable by us as members of the human community. Like a person who tries on a new, more comfortable pair of shoes in preference to an ill-fitting pair of old ones, I feel that we may be collectively "trying on" new elements in our system to accommodate the changes that we need. It comforts me to know that no matter what I may write here, these changes are occurring. I like to think that I've played the role of a journalist, recording my observations, as the transformation of our society takes place. My sincere hope is that the readers of this book will join me in observing as this remarkable process unfolds.

Chapter I

What Is Codependency?

We attempted to use others—our mates, friends and even our children, as our sole source of identity, value and well-being, and as a way of trying to restore within us the emotional losses of our childhoods.

From Co-Dependents Anonymous
Meeting Format

The primary characteristic of codependent behavior is a need to focus on other people to provide love, affirmation or validation. In addition, codependent behavior is distinguished by an individual's urge to control or influence others. Intense and frequently overwhelming, the need to control is most often accompanied by fears of helplessness, powerlessness and impotency. The term codependency was first used to describe individuals who had developed unhealthy and self-destructive behavior patterns because of their involvement with active alcoholics or chemically dependent persons.[1] While in these relationships, codependents seem to be plagued with intensified feelings of shame, fear and anger; but, because of a compulsion to please and care for the addicted persons, they are unable to express these feelings in a healthy way.[2]

Codependents often care for people who are dependent, are unclear about their own lives and who will ultimately abandon them physically and/or emotionally. In some instances, they can develop an obsession for another person that is like an obsession or compulsion for drugs. When faced with separation from the significant person, a codependent can experience intense fears, at times accompanied by anxiety or panic attacks. The pain of this intensity is actually caused by the childhood fear of being unloved or unwanted by members of one's own family.[3]

Often overly responsible for others, codependents can easily become over-extended and can lose interest in their own lives. Inured to their own feelings, they often have difficulty discerning their own wants and needs.[4] Other codependent behavior patterns are difficulty in forming or maintaining close or intimate relationships, perfectionism, rigid behavior and attitudes and difficulties in adjusting to change.[5]

Codependents have difficulty with self-esteem. At one extreme self-esteem is low or nonexistent: the individual thinks she/he is less than others. At the opposite extreme can be arrogance and grandiosity: the individual thinks she/he is set apart and superior to others.[6] Whereas caregivers can give their children the message that they are "less than" others, at other times, children can be taught to find fault with others; they can have a false sense of superiority and believe that they can do no wrong.[7] Both of these individuals have an inner reality which is shame-based.

Children who suffer from low self-esteem are often taught by their parents to feel helpless and incompetent. They are taught that they can do nothing right or should continue trying harder even when their effort is already above average. In a final insult, parents criticize their children for developing the very dependency that they originally taught to them. When children in such families object to their treatment, they often become brainwashed into thinking, feeling and reacting in ways that are only in agreement with their parents' restricted views.[8]

Since they can find no way to please their parents, many children just stop trying and learn to respond to life's challenges with helplessness. They retain these feelings of helplessness in relationships; in response to it they can attempt to exert control over others in either a passive or a domineering manner, depending on her or his conditioning.

In the dysfunctional family spoken and unspoken rules prevent healthy communication. Some rules demand that family members not express feelings openly, or confront problems indirectly. Other injunctions may require a family member or members to be over-achievers, always act in an unselfish manner and be overly respectful to parental authority figures.[9]

Cultural demands to get along with others and to be "nice" only help to compound codependent behaviors. Supported by our educational and religious institutions, our parents have taught us to do what we are told to do and to do it well, to be passive, rather than pushy, and to find satisfaction in helping others solve problems. When we make contact with others we may have inner voices telling us messages such as: Don't be selfish; be reasonable; never lose your cool; don't say anything to hurt others' feelings; help your friends with their problems; be thoughtful of those in pain; always be nice.[10]

Being nice helps us to gain others' support; it saves us from criticism, embarrassment and rejection. Traits such as consideration and courtesy have helped to create a humane society, but we, as individuals, can pay a very high price, if we over-indulge in them.[11] Obsessively "nice" people are often out of touch with their own wants, needs and desires. Unable to feel their feelings, they are often depressed, anxious, or suffer from somatic complaints. Because of their low self-esteem and inability to be direct, "nice" people have difficulty in sustaining close, trusting relationships.

Codependents learn to engage in relationships that are unequal in nature. Although they give to others, they often get little back in return. When relationships, plans or jobs do not work out as planned, the codependent often feels depressed, bitter or angry. Often the codependent will blame her or himself by asking questions such as, "What did I do wrong?", or, "How did I fail?" At other times, she or he will blame others, asking questions such as, "Why did they do this to me?"[12]

The low self-worth of the codependent is more pervasive than simply the habit of comparing oneself unfavorably with others; it can be a deep, underlying feeling that, "I'm not worth it." Codependents believe that they are not worth the choices they need to make, the job they deserve to have, or the healthy relationships they would like. Ironically, they frequently don't believe they are worth the effort it would take to get out of the painful situations they often find themselves in.[13]

The codependent will often remain in unhealthy relationships or settings, despite numerous warnings that the situation is unworkable. Overly loyal and essentially insecure, the codependent resists change and can tolerate unhealthy situations for protracted periods of time. She or he may presume that no matter how bad their situation is, the known present is better than the unknown future.

Children of dysfunctional families are not only taught by their parents that they have to be perfect, but that the standards for perfection are out of reach. Fearing that they can't measure up, children nevertheless continue to fruitlessly seek approval from their parents, often attempting to gain it in other ways. Eventually, the approval-seeking behavior generalizes to relationships with teachers, friends and employers; it refers to a deep-seated, private and often unconscious belief that the road to love, belonging, acceptance and success is dependent on our ability to do what we think others want or expect us to do.[14]

Codependents can experience extensive problems with communication. In living with another's addictive or dysfunctional behavior a codependent may have adapted to being lied to, receiving mixed messages or controlling, suppressive and manipulative communication.[15] Because of repression, denial or self-protection, codependents often do not know what it is they want to say or how they want to say it. Often confused, they communicate in ways which are indirect, rather than direct.[16] Unable to express themselves clearly, they can easily feel misunderstood. They may have a great deal of difficulty allowing someone to get close to them or in trusting someone enough to share their true feelings with them. In order to gain the other person's approval, the codependent may say only what they perceive the other person would like to hear.[17]

Unresolved relationship conflicts in early childhood that show up in current relationships will press for a sense of resolution and completion.[18] Individuals who didn't separate adequately from their parents may often feel a need to a return to a state of "oneness" that they may have felt while in a symbiotic relationship with their primary care-giver.[19] Codependency creates the illusion that your mother or father, on whom you counted to make you feel good or safe or secure, now exists in the person with whom you have a relationship. You might hear an individual make statements such as, "I don't feel complete as a person without him/her. She/he makes me feel like a whole person." Or, "I would die if I ever lost her/him. My life wouldn't be worth living. I could never be happy again." Or one might be heard to say, "When I'm not with her/him I feel insecure. When we cuddle up together, I feel really safe." Despite the initial illusion of safety, over the long-term this attitude usually leads to manipulation and control rather than to a loving and long-lasting relationship.[20]

Codependents control for a number of reasons: they control in the name of love, they control out of fear; some control because they feel themselves empowered to do so. Others secretly and covertly manipulate, while hiding behind a facade of niceness. Still others, who play the role of victims, are able to control by appearing helpless or incompetent. They let us know that they need our cooperation badly and can't live without it.[21] Although they are obsessed with the need to be *in* control, codependents ironically experience an intense fear of being *out* of control. It is paradoxical that the more control codependents try to exert over their lives, the more out of control they often feel.[22]

Not feeling loved, codependents often settle for being needed. Rescuing momentarily distracts them from their own inner pain by making them feel competent and useful.[23] A pattern of rescuing can develop quickly into one of caretaking. Those who continuously play the caretaking role can become victims and attract perpetrators. Continually giving more than they receive, codependents often feel abused and neglected. Although they anticipate the needs of others, they wonder why no one notices their needs.[24] One of the best indicators of whether you are codependent depends upon how much your needs are being met by others.[25]

Young women often learn to be caretakers in alcoholic families; unaccustomed to asking for nurturing for themselves, they are socialized to be over-responsible and emotional caretakers for others. They are paradoxically taught to be dependent on others, but not to express their own emotional needs. Adult daughters often perceive themselves as the expressive centers of their families; they are often taught that it is their responsibility to ensure that all family members are under control and emotionally satisfied.[26]

The primary messages communicated to caretaking individuals living in an alcoholic or dysfunctional family are: 1) If I can control everything, I can keep my family from becoming upset. 2) If I please everyone, everyone will be happy. 3) It is my fault, and I am to blame when trouble occurs. 3) It is my responsibility to ensure that everyone in the family gets along with each other. 4) Take care of others first. 5) Expressing anger is not appropriate. 6) I am responsible for the success of a relationship. 7) For something to be acceptable, it must be perfect. 8) I am not a good person.[27]

There is a paradoxical quality to a codependent's existence. Although she/he exhibits many of the skills necessary to survive and even thrive in the world, these skills are manifested primarily on behalf of others. By and large very competent, many cannot perceive their true worth.

Codependency has frequently been referred to as a disease. Author Pia Mellody, for instance, repeatedly refers to the "symptoms" of this disease which she indicates is rampant in our culture.[28] This concept most likely was created to maintain language similar to the medical model of mental illness originally adopted by Sigmund Freud, the forerunner of the modern mental health movement around the turn of the twentieth century, and his colleagues, all of whom were physicians. In certain instances, such as with the psychosis associated with a physical disease such as syphilis and where there appears to be a genetic predisposition for mental conditions such as depression in certain families, there is evidence for a clear physical cause for a disordered mental condition. In others, however, such as those with various types of neuroses, a physical cause cannot clearly be established. In the latter instances, the term "mental illness" can be used only in a metaphorical sense. Nevertheless, the mental health establishment has routinely maintained the use of this term to describe many behavioral disorders. These behaviors have been given psychiatric labels and have been categorized in a diagnostic manual. One rarely questions today when a disordered behavior is described as an "illness" even if it's clear that the behavior has little in common with actual physical diseases such as cancer or diabetes.

In my opinion codependency is not a disease, but a learned behavior. Psychiatrist and psychoanalyst Thomas Szasz has stated that there is little or no similarity between the problems in living experienced and expressed in terms of the symptoms of mental illness and the symptoms of physical diseases. He has further stated that conditions termed as mental illnesses and their treatments should instead be dealt with as personal, social, and ethical problems in living, rather than as synonymous with physical illness.[29]

As mentioned earlier, Duke Robinson, in his book *Too Nice for Your Own Good,* establishes a connection between codependent behaviors and our culture's expectations. In books specifically addressing codependency, however, such admissions are rare. In a review of seven books about codependency only two mentioned a strong connection between culture and codependency. In his seminal work about codependency, for instance, Robert Subby describes the primary source of codependency is in from the "troubled family system."[30] Pia Mellody states that codependency stems from the "painful aftermath of experiencing childhood in a dysfunctional family.[31] Although in her books, *Codependent No More* and *Beyond Codependency*, Melody Beattie does not name a central cause or causes for codependency, she focuses almost entirely on stories and examples regarding relationships. Thus, the reader must assume that she views the cause of codependency as stemming primarily from unhealthy relationships. Although it does not attempt to diagnose codependency, the "Big Book" of Co-Dependents Anonymous states in its meeting format, that codependence "is born out of our sometimes moderately or sometimes extremely dysfunctional family systems."[32] In contrast, in their book, *Breaking Free from the Codependent Trap*, Weinhold and Weinhold provide an in-depth explanation for codependent behaviors as stemming from our civilization's adoption of a "dominator" model of society, which tends to maintain rankings between individuals, thus inhibiting the development of equality in relationships.[33] In their book, *Against the Wall: Men's Reality in a Codependent Culture*, authors Hardy and Hough use the term "parental culture" to describe the cultural influence which provides a background of values against which we judge our lives and ourselves.[34] Although their work focuses mostly on the male experience, only the latter two authors mention gender conditioning in connection with codependent behavior.[35]

Challenging Codependency – Feminist Critiques, edited by Marguerite Babcock and Christine McKay is composed of a series of essays by professional women who've worked in mental health settings and who've explored the relationship of gender conditioning with codependency for women. Viewing these behaviors primarily within a political and economic context, the authors consider it inappropriate for these patterns to be addressed within a mental health or a twelve-step recovery setting. The authors are critical of twelve-step recovery movements, especially Co-Dependents Anonymous, for unnecessarily treating as pathological the behavior of women who play the traditional female role.

Many codependents address their problems in individual or group psychotherapeutic settings. However, one of the most common ways that codependents have sought relief from their inner conflicts has been through the twelve-step recovery program of Co-Dependents Anonymous, adapted from the twelve-step program originated by Alcoholics Anonymous. Participation in this program is voluntary, and the only condition for membership in it is a desire for healthy and fulfilling relationships. Although the majority of those who attend Co-dependents Anonymous meetings regularly are self-identified codependents, I strongly suspect that there are countless others not in attendance who suffer from this disordered behavior pattern, but who cannot or will not identify themselves as being a part of this group.

Chapter 2

Coming Out

And there was a new voice that kept you company
as you strode deeper and deeper into the world,
determined to save the only life you could save.
                                    Mary Oliver

Codependents often live their lives vicariously through those they attempt to control. Although sensitive to others' needs, they are paradoxically out of touch with their own. Other features of codependency are low self-esteem, perfectionism, rigidity, and avoidance of conflict.[1] Books and literature available on the subject emphasize that the pattern is caused primarily by being raised in a dysfunctional family. Although gender and cultural conditioning have been peripherally mentioned in connection with it, codependency is widely considered to be an individual problem.[2]

Almost from the very beginning I perceived my experience as a codependent to be more complex than the "individual problem" just described. After attending meetings of Co-dependents Anonymous for less than a year, I began to sense the profound influence that my upbringing as a woman had contributed to my codependency. Growing up in the 50's and

60's, I had learned that my primary role as a woman was to serve my family, which included my husband, children and parents. I was raised to be a housewife, a mother, a helpmate and caregiver, all very necessary but culturally under-valued roles. I was taught that the man in my life would be the primary breadwinner and the dominant member of our relationship. Men that I knew were often involved with endeavors considered "important," such as earning income and taking care of family finances. As heads of households, they were perceived as the true managers of the family. When I grew up, men dominated the working world. In those days it was unusual to see physicians, religious leaders, journalists or business professionals who were women.

My parents encouraged me to be feminine and lady-like. I was taught not to directly express anger or frustration. I was a quiet, good child, and my passive ways were encouraged by my parents; I learned to listen respectfully to others, especially to adults, and even to boyfriends of my age. While in their company, I learned not to focus too much on myself. Instead, I was encouraged to focus my attention on them. Subjected to this conditioning over many years, it was not surprising that I became an inveterate "people pleaser." Pleasing others was the only way I knew how to gain love and support from my family and friends. At the age of eighteen, after graduating from high school and feeling unclear about my professional goals, I attended a two-year girls' college which was surrounded by all-male colleges. It was not until later that I fully realized that I had attended that school in large part to obtain my "Mrs." Degree.

While I was raised to be a "typical" female of that time, other aspects of my upbringing were far from typical. By the time I had reached middle school, I was being verbally abused on a regular basis by my alcoholic father. The feelings of anxiety, depression and low self-esteem I experienced as a consequence made it difficult for me to establish and maintain healthy relationships; this was particularly true in my relationship with my father. Although I desperately wanted his love and support, after continuously being subjected to his verbal attacks, I eventually lost the ability to feel comfortable or trusting while in his presence. My mother was unable to defend me against my father's attacks. She would minimize them and encouraged me to be stoic. Although I always loved and admired my mother, where my father was concerned, she would say nothing in my defense, rather than risk his anger.

When not drinking, my father was a quiet and shy man, who preferred reading to the company of others. He was emotionally detached from all of us, except for my mother, whom he adored. It was not until several years later that I learned that my father had suffered verbal abuse from his father, who, I strongly suspect, must have begun verbally attacking him when he was a very young boy.

My father's case was not unusual. After examining the family histories of perpetrators it has been established that many first experience abuse as victims. In the case of our family the abuse was most likely handed down from one generation to the next, along with the unbending expectation of male domination.

Unsurprisingly, I was unable to develop a healthy, loving relationship with a man. When I did marry in my early twenty's, it was to a man, who, like my father, was emotionally unavailable. Nevertheless, I helped to put my husband through law school, while working in a clerical job that I disliked intensely. We developed problems in our relationship and, after ten years of marriage, decided to divorce.

My subsequent relationships with men were all replays, in one form or another of the one I had with my father. In some instances, the man drank heavily or alcoholically. In another, he would be emotionally detached or abandoning. In a third, he would be physically abusive. None of these men wanted to seriously change in any way through a recovery program, therapy or counseling. It would take eighteen years from the date of divorce from my first husband before I could finally establish a healthy relationship with a man, one characterized by caring, love and mutual respect.

In those early years my primary role was one of sacrifice. Since I had learned that sacrifice was central to my role as a woman, this conditioning was very difficult for me to overcome. It was an entrenched behavior in me, and it would be decades before I learned to not over-extend myself for the sake of others. One unfortunate by-product of my upbringing was that, although I was expected to give to others, I was not to expect to get back from those I had given to. My golden rule read: Give unto others but expect nothing back from them.

I learned many of these beliefs and behaviors through exposure to my Protestant Church's doctrine. After I had been in recovery for only a short period of time, I began to perceive Christianity as a philosophy that confused healthy self-love with selfishness. Although the leaders of my church would encourage its members to love their neighbors as themselves, they were never able to explicitly state that self-love *by itself* could be a valuable and worthwhile pursuit. We were taught that we could love ourselves only within the context of selfless "Christian" devotion; it was better to give rather than to receive. The Church's doctrines also reinforced the belief that the primary role for women was marriage and childbearing. It emphasized that the "natural" caretaking qualities inherent in the roles of wife and motherhood represented Christ-like love and should be encouraged in women. Ironically, it would be these "spiritual" qualities that I would question after reviewing my personal history, where I had been both victimized and abused.

My professional development was severely restricted by a curious admixture of family and cultural expectations. Because I had been taught from a young age that marriage and family were the only roles seriously available to me, I approached my work life casually, drifting from one job to the next. The men I gravitated towards during this period seemed disinterested in marriage and children; I failed to establish a stable relationship with any of them. Nonetheless, in trying to obtain my domestic dream, I continued in my attempts to fulfill this quixotic illusion until I was past the age of 40. Eventually, one day, my house of cards came crashing down. I found myself caught between my child-like world of faded ideals and the harsh, unflinching light of reality, unable to achieve either my dream of home and family, or the financial stability and status that a stable career could have afforded me.

As a codependent, I had not learned how to take care of myself; many of my decisions were self-defeating. At one point, although I had wanted to pursue a graduate degree, I decided against moving to a city where, at the local university, I could have pursued a meaningful career. Instead, I remained with my former husband, as he refused to leave the city where we were then living. By sacrificing my goals for his, as a "good wife," I was left with the option of studying for a degree which had only limited possibilities for advancement. Later, because of a series of economic downturns, the types of positions that I did qualify for with this degree were eventually eliminated. By short-circuiting my professional development in such ways, I made misguided decisions that have had negative consequences for me into the present.

Seeming to copy my family history, my work settings were often unstable, abusive or abandoning. At work I often found myself stepping into professional "mud-puddles." After reviewing this pattern in later years, I realized that the set of emotional expectations that I had developed from my father had not only generalized to my personal relationships, but to authority figures in work settings. After more than four decades of learning subordinate behavior patterns, not only had I been unable to achieve appropriate developmental milestones, but I had difficulty learning behaviors that would help me to take care of myself either on a personal or professional basis.

After attending Co-Dependents Anonymous meetings for a few years, I began to realize that although an exaggerated form, the codependent behaviors I had developed growing up in my dysfunctional family were an extension of the behavior patterns I had learned from my conditioning as a woman. The subordinate "pleasing" pattern that I had learned growing up in my home seemed to be part of a carefully crafted feminine role that I had been socialized to play, not only by my family, but by the traditions of my culture. All the other girls in my class at school had received the same messages that I had. These messages came to us from many sources: school, church, workplace and home, and would dove-tail, each reinforcing the others. We were being groomed, first and foremost, to be good wives and mothers. For most of us career pursuits or personal ambitions were either put on the back burner or abandoned altogether.

My need to understand how my upbringing as a woman had contributed to my codependency became insatiable. I read books on codependency, gender, psychology and sociology. I learned about dysfunctional families. I researched works by feminists and feminist-theologians. I began to understand that the genesis of codependent behavior for women and men would be found in the traditional gender roles that had evolved through the centuries, roles which had always been considered "normal" by our cultural standards. Because of their longevity these roles had an entrenched quality, were resistant to change and were reinforced by a variety of authority figures in our social institutions.

I began to write. In the beginning I wrote in journals, expressing my feelings about my life, relationships and family life. Later, I began to write about the ideas that had been introduced to me from the books I had read. Although it was a gradual process, I could not stop asking questions, nor could I learn enough. Although I had discovered two authors who had dealt with the subject of gender and codependency, their work appeared to be largely ignored or marginalized.

I had never written professionally; nor had I ever imagined doing so. Nevertheless, I began to consider writing a book. At first, I had trouble believing what my mind was telling me. And so, I waited. I waited for the shoe to drop. I waited for someone to tell me to stop writing. I waited for my book to be written by someone else. I waited to be relieved of this looming responsibility. But none of these things happened. No one else wrote my book, and no one told me to stop writing. Incredibly, I found that the responsibility remained mine alone.

I experienced strong and protracted periods of self-doubt which filled me with dread and ambivalence. The task seemed overwhelming. I could not conceive of ever finishing it. Repeatedly, I examined my motives. At one point I reasoned that if we all had survived patriarchy for 6,000 years, who was I to question it? Weren't we all doing fine, after all? But during periods of contemplation, a quiet but persistent inner voice would answer my question. The answer I always heard was, "No."

Although exciting for me, for others, the topic of gender could be rife with conflicts and unspoken taboos. I was afraid of upsetting anyone. Conditioned to be a "good" (you fill in the blank) sister, daughter, person, family member, wife, woman, student, etc., I was desperately afraid of offending anyone, especially male authority-figures, by reporting unpleasant facts that might upset them, even if these facts happened to be true. The possibility of disturbing any of these distant individuals with my writing filled me with a fear so intense that it required me to tap into pockets of courage and inner resources that I had never thought I possessed. But, who were these individuals, really? I would ask myself. The answer was always the same: It was *them* -- the collection of anonymous, faceless, impersonal (often male) authority figures that I had spent my entire adult life pleasing. By facing the possibility of upsetting even one of them, I had to break one of my cardinal rules: *Always* play it safe. I had always gotten through life by following this dictum. By writing material about gender relations for possible publication, I was most definitely *not* playing it safe. What in the world had I been thinking of?

I had many fears. I feared that by examining gender relations, my writing could confuse some people, while making others feel threatened or vulnerable. I feared that my writing would create self-doubt in both men and women. Few like to have their lives shaken up and examined. I reasoned that it would be too difficult for many, as most people are busy just surviving. I feared that my motives would be misunderstood, and that some would feel that I was favoring one gender over the other. But, finally, I reasoned that there might be others, like me, who could use this knowledge. And so, I continued with my research.

One of the most difficult aspects of my research was the ambivalence that we as a society have about examining gender relations. After generations of conditioning many of us view our traditional gender roles as "normal," despite our awareness of the conflicts imbedded within them. In families and close circles most men and women care about each other; we're brothers and sisters, husbands and wives, colleagues, neighbors and sometimes, even best friends. Most of us just want to just do the "right thing," without making waves. In the absence of alternative viewpoints or insights, we tend to revert to the "default" conditioning of our childhoods, where inequalities or conflicts were presented to us as "normal" by the adults around us. By questioning these standards, we take the risk of being viewed as outlanders by our communities and social circles. This is a risk that few can easily assume.

Yet this was the risk that I had to face. After discussing the issue with a number of individuals, many justified our gender inequality because of tradition. Although understandable, I found this argument to be both circular and spurious. I strongly believed then, as I do today, that although our traditional gender roles may reflect what we're used to, they do not even begin to address what we're truly capable of as human beings.

I believed that men and women were fundamentally equal. Yet, even after extensive research, this simple premise seemed hopelessly convoluted. I found that relations between the genders are often affected by a see-saw-like pattern. As men become elevated, women are devalued. Conversely, elevating women seems to have the opposite effect, of making men feel less valuable as men. To make matters worse, our gender system seemed to be entrenched, creating a perpetual, either/or polarity between the sexes.

Since true equality between the sexes was difficult to quantify, I looked for a measure not unlike equivalency, which seemed to exist between the male and female of other species. Although the male and female of a particular species may play different roles, they are, nonetheless, equivalent, when weighing the total contributions of the members of that sex to the life of the group of which they belong. One can see equivalency most clearly in the relationships between males and females of species such as African lions, the emperor penguins of Antarctica, and the bonobo chimpanzees of Africa. Yet, even though we can observe gender relations of another animal species with a certain degree of objectivity, it is much more difficult to do the same while observing our own. Nevertheless, it was just this type of objectivity that I hoped to achieve. An inveterate idealist, I wanted to state my ideas and perceptions in an unbiased manner. This was easier said that done. Memories and feelings kept getting in the way. Frustrated, I would take breaks from writing to deal with them. I would return when I felt more detached. Frequently, I'd asked myself if it was possible for me or anyone else to be completely objective about gender. I really didn't know. All I could do was to try.

I began to understand that over thousands of years our social structure had evolved in response to real needs of the communities which had created it. But how was it that our *particular* type of society had evolved? Why was it that while we aggrandized war we paradoxically extolled the virtues of home and family? I wondered why women, who I understood to be equivalent to men in over-all intellectual ability, were so often subordinate to them in the workplace. I wondered why little boys are allowed to cry, but not grown men. I wondered why childcare and care-giving were tasks that had traditionally been considered appropriate only for women.

In order to better understand our culture's gender roles, I decided to study the history of pre-patriarchal cultures which had preceded it. I had a very personal reason for doing this. Because my father's power over me had seemed inextricably connected to the fact that he was the patriarch of our family, I, as the middle of his three daughters, was near the lowest rung in relationship to him. This belief was reinforced by my family, my religion, as well as other individuals in my life, such as distant relatives, friends and teachers. The structure of my family did not encourage me to object to, question or even struggle against this arrangement. I tolerated this behavior without complaint for many years. When I began a twelve-step recovery program in my late 40's, however, I began to realize that the major lesson that I had learned from this experience was how to tolerate abuse. Although I understood how to react to crises, I had no idea how to handle my problems in a proactive or assertive manner. I had little confidence. I was burdened with low self-esteem and an inordinate amount of guilt and self-blame. In the terms of the twelve-step recovery program, I had "bottomed out."

In examining my situation, I asked myself some obvious questions: How had I arrived at this place? What structures had contributed to my current situation? And, more importantly, how could I escape from them? In order to deal effectively with the emotions of my past, to detach and move on, I felt compelled to understand more about the belief structure that, after generations of patriarchy, had led me tolerate the abuse not only within my own family, but, in a much larger sense, within my own culture. I believed that without this insight into my own culture's past, I would forever remain a victim: silent, powerless and filled with shame and self-doubt.

The more questions I was able to answer, the more I asked. I was, however, able to understand one important truth. In examining the structure of patriarchy, I came to understand that it was a social institution that we as a society had created in order to help us to survive. Since we *have* survived as a people, obviously, patriarchy has done its job. It will continue to do so as long as we need it to. However, somewhere during this process we've forgotten that, as a society, patriarchy is *our* creation; we are not *its* creation. Somewhere in its evolution it took on a life of its own. Like Hal, the computer in the movie *2001,* at some point, it stopped being under *our* control, and *it* started to control *us.*

As an institution that we helped to create, patriarchy is changing and evolving to meet our needs. These changes sometimes seem slow and glacial. And yet in many areas across our globe, such as in North America, Western Europe and Australia, they have been occurring quite rapidly, especially over the past fifty years. Some welcome these changes with open arms, whereas others feel threatened by them. For those nostalgic for the way things used to be, I am

Elizabeth Ralston

often reminded of a conversation I had with a middle-aged woman from a conservative Christian background who was still smarting from years of mistreatment from a long-term relationship with an abusive man. After sharing her story with me, she summarized her viewpoint with one simple statement: "We women cannot go back again."

I resisted examining my gender conditioning, until, like a fish swimming upstream against the current, I felt overwhelmed by the sheer magnitude of its presence. As a recovering codependent it was no longer enough for me to examine my relationship to my family alone. My grandparents, parents, aunts, uncles, extended family all learned how to behave within a social context, and so had I. In order to become healthier, I had to examine my relationship to society as a woman.

While writing this book, I was also struck with the understanding that if I was to write about gender, I would have to write about both sexes. It was clear to me then, as it is now, that the problem of gender between men and women involves the quality of the *relationship* between them. Although I didn't know if I could adequately describe this relationship, I knew that I had to try. As feminist scholar Carol Gilligan has written, "Both sexes suffer when one is not understood."[3]

Our stereotyped gender roles call for different behaviors for each of the sexes. Men tend to take the role of the dominant individual, or *manager*, whereas women tend to play the role of the non-dominant individual, or *mother*. Although mothers can be managers to children or to women of lesser status, they are rarely encouraged to be managers of men, unless the men are significantly more subordinate in ability and/or education. As our society's institutions remain male-dominated, for women numerous messages emphasizing established gender roles tend to reinforce one another.

Not long after beginning my recovery as a codependent, I was introduced to the Twelve Promises of Co-Dependents Anonymous. I was amazed by the quietly subversive, but empowering message of Promise Six: "New and renewed relationships are to be with equal partners."[4] I realized that, although I had rarely experienced a truly equal relationship, I knew that I very much wanted to experience one. I reasoned that if I was to become responsible for myself, I had to relate to others as equals. I couldn't simply regress back to being a subordinate. Nor could I dominate others, a role that I had learned, after years of suffering because of it, to reject. I reasoned that developing equal relationships with others would not only give me the chance to develop a healthy autonomy, but it would in turn, enable me to respect the autonomy of others.

I'm constantly reminded of the fact that most women of my generation learned to detach from our traditional roles because we had no choice. The self-abnegating mannerisms of my paternal grandmother wouldn't get me or any other women very far in today's workplaces. Women have much to gain by working to undo the system that oppresses them, not only for themselves in the short run, but for the sake of future generations of women.[5]

Most men, on the other hand, don't realize the impoverishment to their emotional and spiritual lives, the price they pay in personal authenticity, how they compromise their humanity, how they limit the connections they can have with other people, how they distort their sexuality to live up to core patriarchal values of control. . . So, the first thing men can begin to reclaim is their sense of aliveness and realness,

Elizabeth Ralston

their connection to themselves and the world—which they may not even realize was missing until they begin to feel its return.[6]

For all of us, dealing with these changes requires courage. Yet, I believe these transitions are inevitable. Women and men are beginning to demand and expect from themselves and each other an acknowledgement of their shared humanity. One of the first areas of change will be in the area of culturally based codependency which automatically ranks individuals into either dominant or subordinate status. In contrast, relationships established with linking, rather than on a ranked system, would encourage relationships based on cooperative interdependence. Individuals in interdependent relationships work in supportive, cooperative and egalitarian ways; rigid ranking is unnecessary because domination and fear are not the cornerstones to maintaining the structure of the relationship. Those operating interdependently use cooperative 'you and me' thinking, will utilize fluid sex roles, treat diversity non-judgmentally and will share equally in the risk-taking, responsibility, investment, means of production, rewards, labor and support.[7]

To accept yourself as a full human being, you must acknowledge that your good qualities, whether they're thought of as feminine or masculine are fine for you. . . . In order to do this, ingrained notions of masculinity and femininity must be challenged.[8] Men could learn to recreate themselves as human beings capable of experiencing attitudes such as empathy and caring and feelings such as fear and grief. Women, on the other hand, could exhibit healthy assertiveness and pursue personal ambitions without fear of being branded as selfish, self-serving or overly aggressive. Most importantly, men and women could learn to care for one another as equals and friends, developing true partnerships, without fearing that by doing so they might compromise their standing as members of their respective genders.

As we expand beyond the cultural envelopes that we inhabit, my hope is that we can free ourselves from the restrictions of our gender roles. By doing so we can achieve our unique potentials and truly experience our shared humanity. As Allan Johnson has pointed out, "As our inner and outer lives become less bound by the strictures of fear and compromise, we can claim a deeper meaning for our lives than we've known before."[9]

Chapter 3

A Brief History

What will the writing of history be like, when that umbrella of dominance is removed and definition is shared equally by men and women? Will we devalue the past, overthrow the categories, supplant order with chaos?

No—we will simply step out under the free sky. We will observe how it changes, how the stars rise and the moon circles, and will describe the earth and its workings in male and female voices.

The Creation of Patriarchy
By Gerda Lerner

As I researched this book, I was struck with an understanding which has been instrumental in my recovery from codependency. That assumption was that from the perspective of nature, the feminine principle (of which I was a representative) was equivalent to the masculine in overall importance and function. Any concepts of superiority or inferiority of one gender over another were put in place because of the economic, political and religious needs of our social system. Influenced by the traditions of our culture, these beliefs colored and distorted our collective reality in order to maintain that culture. Nature did not create them. It became clear to me that I had to examine carefully any belief, cultural or otherwise, that restricted my recovery from codependency. In order to examine our culture's beliefs about gender, I wanted to begin with the history of these beliefs, to understand how they had developed and how they had changed over time. Since none of us matures in a vacuum, I hoped that an examination of our cultural history would help me to increase my understanding of how the structure of our society has shaped our collective lives. I came to understand that, although it has been traditionally characterized as perennial and unchanging, our society's structure has not always been as it is now. Changes have been the norm, not the exception, and some of its most profound changes have occurred in recent decades.

I began my research with the study of cultures that pre-dated Classical Greece and Judeo-Christian societies. Because there is much that is not known about these societies, I've attempted as much as possible to present material about them which has been derived from archeological and other historical evidence.

Pre-Judeo-Christian Societies

In a study of art found in sixty caves in France, Andre Leroi-Gourhan, author of one of the most important studies of Paleolithic art, hypothesized that the art found in these caves expressed some form of early religion in which feminine representations and symbols played a central part.[1] Among his observations, Leroi-Gourhan noted that the female figures

Elizabeth Ralston

and the symbols interpreted as feminine were located in a central position in the excavated chambers, whereas the masculine symbols typically either occupied peripheral positions or were arranged around the female figures and symbols.[2]

Similarly, numerous female figurines and sculptures, made of stone, bone and clay have been found in areas where small settled communities had once existed. These sculptures, some dating back as far as 25,000 BC, have been found in Gravettian-Aurignacian sites from the Upper Paleolithic Age in areas as far apart as Spain, France, Germany, Austria, Czechoslovakia and Russia. The sites and figures appear to span a period of at least 10,000 years.[3]

Historical evidence from the fourth millennium forward, derived from myths, rituals and creation stories indicate that the Mother-Goddess is virtually universal as the dominant figure in the most ancient stories.[4] The Great Mother seems to have been the most sacred figure of the pre-patriarchal period; she ruled over both life and death, and was worshiped simultaneously as Mother Goddess, mistress of the animals and receiver of the dead.[5] This Goddess worship survived well into historic times. It is found in the worship of well-known deities such as Isis, Nut and Maat in Egypt; Ishtar, Astarte, and Lilith in the Fertile Crescent, Demeter, Kore and Hera in Greece and Atargatis, Ceres and Cybele in Rome, . . . in the Shekhina of Hebrew kabalistic tradition, and in the Catholic Virgin Mary, considered to be the Mother of God.[6]

Tremendous reverence was paid to the Goddess over a period of between seven thousand to twenty-five thousand years ago; hers was a religion which held widespread power as well as extreme longevity. She was considered to be the giver of life and all that promotes fertility, and at the same time she was the wielder of the destructive powers of nature. The feminine nature. . .is light as well as dark.[7] The Great Goddess was regarded as immortal, changeless, omnipotent, and the concept of fatherhood had not yet been introduced into religious thought.[8] Though at first, the Goddess appears to have reigned alone, at some unknown point in time, she had precedence over the young god, with whom she was associated as her son, husband or lover.[9]

Of two Neolithic archeological sites discovered by James Mellaart in the 1960's in modern-day Turkey, Catal Huyuk was a ceremonial center for the goddess religion.[10] Peace-loving societies, Catal Huyuk and another Neolithic society unearthed, Hacilar, show no evidence of damage through warfare of spans of over fifteen hundred years.[11]

After thousands of years of patriarchal heritage, it's often difficult to conceive of a society led by women as anything other than being the opposite of a patriarchy, or a matriarchy. In reality, these earlier societies appear to have operated from a different paradigmatic framework. Although the lines of succession were matrilineal, with property being passed down from mother to daughter, little evidence suggests that females in these earlier cultures dominated men, as women were dominated by men in later, patriarchal societies. In sites unearthed from Neolithic-Chalcolithic southeastern Europe of circa 7000 and 3500 B.C.E., the archeological evidence suggests a basically equalitarian society with few marked distinctions based on either class or sex. In her studies of these old European societies, archaeologist Marija Gimbutas writes of an equalitarian male-female society. This is demonstrated in part by the fact that there was little difference in wealth of equipment discernible between male and female graves.[12]

Elizabeth Ralston

The fact that women played a central role in prehistoric religion and life does not mean that men were perceived and treated as subservient. As Eisler points out, these social organizations cannot be called matriarchal or patriarchal; instead they seem to resemble partnerships, societies in which neither major group is ranked over the other, and which diversity is not equated with inferiority or superiority.[13]

Ruins of peaceful goddess-worshipping societies have also been found on the islands of Malta and Crete. From the evidence of the ruins, these ancient societies each maintained at least one thousand years of culture unbroken by war.[14] In a 1992 Canadian documentary entitled, *Goddess Remembered*, it was reported that among the ruins of Crete, no armed fortifications had ever been found.

Women were among the first healers of the ancient world. From archaeological excavations in Iraq it has been discovered that the Sumerians, and not the ancient Greeks, were the parents of Western healing systems. Until about 2000 B.C., women participated fully in sacred activities, owned property and businesses and, if they were unmarried, could serve as priestess/physicians.[15] In Old Europe, women were shamans and healers in the Danish culture of the time. Tacitus, a Roman who wrote of the Northern peoples, observed that they "believe that there resides in women an element of holiness and prophecy, and so they do not scorn to ask their advice or lightly disregard their replies."[16] Beginning about 2000 B.C. in ancient Greece women were renowned as healers. Worshipping a pantheon of goddesses of healing such as Demeter, Persephone, Hecate and Hera, women such as those from the Asclepius family were instrumental in initiating our present Western tradition of medicine. Living around 900 B.C., it is from the members of this family that the

Hippocratic Oath of honor, recited by modern-day physicians, is attributed. The physician Asclepius, his daughters Hygeia (representing prevention) and Panacea (representing cure), as well as his wife Epione, who became the patron-saint for those in pain. Each woman in the Aslepius family had her own caduceus—the snake-entwined staff that today is the symbol for medicine.[17]

Three main themes appear to dominate our understanding of these earlier civilizations: 1. Respect for women seems to be evident in these earlier cultures; it is not known, however, to what degree this trend was universal among all classes of women. 2. Many of these societies appear to be cooperative and egalitarian in nature, with fewer divisions among social classes and groups than was found in later, more war-like cultures. 3. Finally, the evidence suggests that many of these communities were extraordinarily peace-loving, some with periods of over one thousand years unbroken by war.

Advent of Patriarchy

By Five Thousand BCE, or about seven thousand years ago, archaeological evidence indicate clear signs of stress and disruption of the old Neolithic in many territories. There is evidence of invasions, natural catastrophes, and sometimes both, causing large-scale destruction and dislocation.[18] As a result of invasions by nomadic tribes, the pottery and sculptural art of Old Europe's incipient civilization quickly vanished.[19] Names for these groups familiar to historians are the Aryans in India, Hittites in the Middle East, Luwians in Anatolia, Kurgans in eastern Europe, Achaeans in Greece, and the Hebrews in Canaan.[20] Only around the Aegean and on the islands did the ancient traditions survive to the end of the third millennium B.C., and on Crete to the mid-second millennium B.C.[21]

Ruled by warriors and priests, these societies worshipped male gods of war. Political forms were changed and economic and social forms shifted, creating stratification of classes. Women fell in status. Widespread warfare, enslavement of human beings and human sacrifice began to bloody the Middle East. Social stratification led to classes of the very rich and the very poor.[22]

The one thing these groups had in common was a dominator model of social organization. A social system in which males dominated through warfare and other forms of social violence through a hierarchic and authoritarian social structure played a central role in diverting our cultural evolution from one based on partnership to one based on domination.[23] To accomplish this, adherents of power—priests, soldiers—had to teach men to dominate and have contempt for women (as well as most men). Throughout this process, men were not only isolated from women, but from values associated with women.[24]

In order to accomplish this transformation, basic changes occurred in the dissemination of information. Only behaviors, attitudes and perceptions that conformed with dominator values were encouraged; information required to create and sustain a society with these values was spread throughout the various communities.[25] Once early societies began resorting to warfare, it was likely others they came into contact with were either decimated or learned to fight back in kind. Eventually, even those cultures which had originally been peace-loving had to adopt war-like strategies and militaristic world views in order to survive. Over thousands of years myths and belief systems were re-written, and goddesses were exchanged for gods who could lead their people to conquer in times of war. Eventually, warfare became a way of life for all but the most isolated societies. Influenced by a military paradigm, hierarchical structures infiltrated into all social institutions, even to the family.

Masculine dominator values are evident in the Old Testament. In one of the two versions of the Creation, the writers of the Book of Genesis create doubt that women were even created by God. Although a few women are mentioned as having a respected or heroic role in the Old Testament, these are quite overwhelmed by the many more women described in servile, submissive or subordinate roles.[26]

A return to the affirmation of feminine values occurred in the New Testament with the story of the life and teachings of Jesus of Nazareth in the New Testament. Jesus instituted a philosophy of love, gentleness, compassion and mutual responsibility instead of the Old Testament values of toughness, aggressiveness and dominance. He mingled freely and openly with women, engaged in public dialogue with them and ministered to them in public. In doing this he deviated radically from the norms of his time, where male rabbis rarely spoke to women in any public setting. Jesus was accompanied by women in his travels and some of these women served as financial patrons for him and his disciples Most significant of all, each of the New Testament Gospels indicates that it was women who discovered his empty tomb and who were the first to know about and testify to Jesus' resurrection from the dead.[27]

Because of the overwhelming dominance by males in the early Christian Church, however, women lost any vestige of their early status of equality in the Church's early history, which is evidenced numerous times by Paul's letters in

Elizabeth Ralston

the New Testament. By the middle ages, women occupied subordinate positions based on shame; their part in creation was no longer blessed, but cursed.[28]

From 1000 A.D. to 1300 A.D. in medieval Europe, women continued as healers, tending to pregnant women, witnessing the beginning and ending of life, and caring for the sick. They functioned as herbalists and empiricists, sustaining the healing lore through oral tradition and apprenticeship. Most people had access to these wise women, whose medicines and rites were believed to be exceptionally powerful to cure where others could not.[29]

Under the protection and patronage of the ruling classes, a new male-dominated medical profession was eventually created, which coincided with the persecution of female peasants[30] By the thirteenth century European medicine became firmly established as a secular science and a profession which. . . was actively involved in the exclusion of women from the universities and, therefore, their elimination as healers.[31] By the fifteenth century the only profession that women could practice legally was midwifery.[32]

The charge of witchcraft became the most effective means of controlling the monopoly of the healing profession. The official position of the Church was any woman who attempted to cure without having studied medicine must be a witch and must die.[33] The witch threatened the Church in three ways: She was a woman, and not ashamed of it; she appeared to be part of an organized underground of peasant women; and she was a healer whose practice was based in empirical study.[34]

The witch hunts in Europe spanned more than four hundred years, from the fourteenth to the seventeenth centuries, and they were primarily a campaign directed against the female peasant population. The actual number killed will never be known; however, estimates range from two hundred thousand to several million. In Germany alone, one hundred thousand witch burnings were carefully documented.[35]

By the thirteenth century, the institution of marriage had come under control of the Church. Once a secular and civil institution, marriage now disallowed both temporary alliances or divorce. The legal notion of *coverture* was introduced, which prohibited women from having any legal rights whatsoever after they had married, including the right to own property.[36] By the thirteenth century marriage had become an institution that entombed and then erased its female victims, especially in the upper classes.[37]

Pre-industrialized Society

In pre-industrial Europe and colonial America life for the great majority of people had a unity and simplicity which was not found in later in the industrial economy. Men directed the work of the family, introduced their sons to farming or craft work, and sought to maintain harmonious relations within the members of the household. Thus, the home was not only a center of production, but also a system of authority. Under the rule of the father, women had no complex choices to make, no questions as to their nature or destiny: obedience was the rule.[38]

Prior to the shift from the agrarian to the industrial economy both adult men and women were responsible for economic production, as well as family life, including the education and welfare of members of the household. In the early centuries of America, women had a major role in the family's economic production—weaving, sewing, cooking, planting, tending animals and gardens. Their work was integral to the survival of the family. Men worked in or near the homes, were home for meals, worked in close proximity to their children and often directed their activities. There was not a sharp distinction between home and work.[39]

The Changing Concept of Marriage

Prior to the 1800's, marriages took place principally for economic and political reasons. Throughout the period of the Renaissance into the 1700's, however, traditions in Europe gradually changed toward marriages based increasingly on the concepts of love, intimacy and partnership. In sixteenth and seventeenth century Europe, for example, the reason for marriage among the rural populations was not necessarily for the couple to be part of a large extended family unit, but for them to establish their own trade, business or to work their own land. The tendency was to marry later, as in England the median marriage age of young women at that time was 26. Because in rural areas a woman often lacked a dowry, she, as well as her intended, might have to work for several years prior to marriage, often as servants in the homes of the wealthy.[40]

By the early nineteenth century, the idea of marrying for romantic love had gained increasing acceptance. Novels such as those written by the British author Jane Austen, such as *Sense and Sensibility* and *Pride and Prejudice* introduced heroines who were often strong-minded, opinionated and unafraid to speak their minds. The restrictions of the era notwithstanding, these eighteenth-century novels presented a possibility of relationships between men and women based on love, mutual respect and equality.

It was not until the end of the eighteenth century that our modern concept of "the family" emerged. Although it was a family in which the male was ranked in both custom and law over the female, the bonds of mutual affection between husband and wife and between parents and children were increasingly seen as more important than the bonds of authority. The domination of women by men began to be questioned by growing numbers of people, which, in turn led to changes in gender roles, as well as relations between parents and children. As women gained more respect, the role of the mother, as well as a gentle and more loving ideal of parenting became increasingly accepted. Similarly, as young women were able to have more contact with young men, romantic love, rather than parental orders was increasingly accepted as the appropriate basis for marriage.[41]

Family and the Industrial Revolution

The term *breadwinner* was first coined in the early 1800's to describe the responsible family man whose value was equated with his usefulness, service and the recognition of his responsibilities.[42] As the pre-industrial society was replaced by the factory-dominated culture, the workplace became increasingly separated from the home, however. Men now spent their days away from home as breadwinners, a term that would eventually become associated with the nineteenth century's masculine ideal.

In the capitalism of the early nineteenth century, men were not bound to the land, or to their craft traditions, guild memberships, or in dutiful service to employers. In America men were viewed as free to create their own destinies. In this environment of exciting but at times unsettling freedoms, a new term was coined to describe a man who took advantage of this potential for individual achievement, autonomy and wealth: the Self-Made Man. For the manhood of the rising

Elizabeth Ralston

middle class, success must be earned, manhood must be proven constantly.[43]

The proving ground of self-made men would the world of the workplace. Manhood had to be proved in a public arena and in the eyes of other men. From the early nineteenth century to the present day, most of men's efforts to prove their manhood maintain this core element of same-sex social awareness. Sociologist Michael Kimmel has noted: "From fathers and boyhood friends to our teachers, coworkers and bosses, it is the evaluative eyes of other men that are always upon us, watching, judging."[44]

As the daily activities of men and women grew apart, a new view of the world emerged which exaggerated the differences between the spheres of "the world" and "the home." This separation between the world of work and home also separated the ideal for men and women into polarized opposites. Thus, women were expected to provide warmth, nurturance and care and forgo achievement. Men, in contrast, were expected to provide money and success, and forgo close attachments. The ideal of masculinity was self-control, limited displays of affection, no weakness; no excessive self-indulgence in feelings. Encouraged to represent the new feminine ideal, women soon came to exhibit characteristics opposite from those of men.[45]

Man the earner, woman the nurturer thus came to represent the ideal. While some writers urged men to establish closer relationships with their children, the structure of work and the ideology that supported it worked against the strengthening of these bonds.[46] Although men often felt a commitment to establish compassionate relationships with their children, they felt honor-bound to earn an income for their families. Although many felt torn because of the opposition of these roles, as long as fathers identified themselves primarily as breadwinners and focused their lives in the public domain, being the second parent to their children held little importance. The significance of the gender ideology of the day was, consequently, strengthened and confirmed : mothers would dominate the emotional aspects of family life, and fathers, the instrumental.[47] It was in the middle and upper classes where the roles between the genders most strictly diverged. The man was expected to take part in a career in the public sphere, whereas the woman remained at home to have and to raise the children. The assumption was created that men "supported" their wives at home, as if unpaid work were not productive and not part of the "real" economy. As women's labor at home lost status as "work," it was nostalgically celebrated as a "labor of love." In the late eighteenth and early nineteenth centuries the hardworking colonial wife was replaced by the "angel of the hearth,". . . who tended to the spiritual, emotional and physical needs of her brood, leaving the material aspects of life to her husband.[48]

For the upper class woman the tasks of keeping house, cooking and minding the children were given as much as possible to the domestic help. She was specialized for sexual and reproductive duties in return for financial support. A successful man of the time could have no better social ornament than an idle wife. Her delicacy, her culture, her childlike ignorance of the male world gave a man the "class" which money alone could not buy. A virtuous affluent wife spent a hushed and peaceful life indoors sewing, sketching, planning menus, and supervising the servants and children. Because of their enforced idleness, however, women of the upper classes were afflicted with an epidemic of female

Elizabeth Ralston

invalidism that never afflicted the lower class or working class women of the time. . . . [49]

In the late nineteenth century the caretaking role for women within the home was redefined to encompass caring for the needy within the community. Middle-class women correctly perceived that they would be less vulnerable to attacks of being "unwomanly" if they could be active in selfless, unremunerated work. With this is mind, women of the nineteenth and twentieth centuries created and staffed organizations designed to aid the less privileged members of society. They were active in the abolitionist movement and underground railway, the Salvation Army, the nursing profession and settlement houses.[50]

This feminine ideal of the late nineteenth century helped to form our society's ideals and philosophies regarding the true role of women for the coming century. There were endless statements from the late nineteenth century which advocated education for women on the grounds that it would make women better housewives and mothers.[51] Although by the beginning of the twentieth century women began to win some political and legal privileges, such as the right to vote and to attend colleges and universities, Virginia Wolf observed that progress was slow for the women of her time:

> Young women, I would say and please attend, . . . you are, in my opinion, disgracefully ignorant. You have never made a discovery of any sort of importance. You have never shaken an empire or led an army into battle. The plays of Shakespeare are not by you, and you have never introduced a barbarous race to the blessings of civilization. What is your excuse?[52]

In a review of the lives of women of accomplishment during the first half of the twentieth century, the traditional feminine marital role appeared to be incompatible with the pursuit of personal ambitions. Those few women who were able to combine marriage or family with a public role did so only by devising radically innovative domestic arrangements. For the most part these enormously productive women were single, divorced, gay, childless, or within socially anomalous relationships that provided highly unusual amounts of support for their work.[53] Frequently women innovators were raised in families that forcefully encouraged unconventional beliefs and actions. This family pattern was found to be the norm for women such as Susan B. Anthony, Jane Addams and Margaret Thatcher.[54]

Unlike men in social and political movements, women's primary aim was to improve life for themselves and others; they did not aim for personal power. Consequently, they achieved their goals slowly and with difficulty, paying for every success with labor, endurance and every ounce of courage they could muster.[55] As an example, from the beginning of the battle in 1848 women's suffrage took seventy-two years to be achieved; the nineteenth amendment was not passed until August, 1920.[56]

By the mid-twentieth century the feminine problem that "has no name" was described by Betty Friedan in her groundbreaking work, *The Feminine Mystique*. In the 1950's the birthrate in the United States was overtaking that of India, and the average marriage age had dropped precipitously. Friedan described a feminine "mystique" which had taught generations of women that to be truly feminine they should give up careers, higher education, and even political rights.[57] As a writer, Friedan became aware of this "problem" after having interviewed countless women for articles in women's magazines. These women complained of feeling empty, bored, tired and depressed, accompanied with vague feelings of dissatisfaction with themselves and with their lives. Although many were college educated, they had given up any hope of careers for marriage and family. Their complaints were all very similar to each other, and seemed reminiscent to those afflicting the affluent nineteenth-century housewives described in preceding paragraphs. Friedan quoted a young Long Island wife:

> I seem to sleep so much. I don't know why I should be so tired. This house isn't nearly so hard to clean as the cold-water flat we had when I was working. The children are at school all day. It's not the work. I just don't feel alive.[58]

Often the problem was smoothed over with the age-old panaceas: such as the need for more love, inner help, having more children, faith in God. At times the problem was dismissed by telling the women how lucky she was to be a woman. The problem was finally dispensed with by shrugging that there are no solutions: this is what being a woman means, and what is wrong with American women that they can't accept their role gracefully?[59]

Women in the Workplace

Friedan's work provided the philosophical basis for a women's movement that helped to produce a fundamental social reorganization on a scale that has most likely never occurred as rapidly, except perhaps in times of war. Sexual mores, the distinctive dress codes for the two sexes, marital norms, employment rates for women and access to previously male-dominated professions all radically changed over the coming decades. In 1960 only 19 percent of married women with preschool children were employed. By 1995 that figure had climbed to 64 percent.[60] Nearly all of the professions in the United States have seen a substantial rise in the percentage of women in their ranks—even if women remain clustered at the lower levels of most career tracks. From 1960 to 1995, the percentage of physicians who were women rose from 9 to 25 percent, while women lawyers increased from 5 to 26 percent of the profession.[61]

Economic influences helped to create enormous changes in the workplace. In the late 1970's and early 1980's a severe recession caused the loss of thousands of manufacturing jobs as large companies closed plants and downsized their operations. Nationwide these plan shutdowns and relocations cost 11.5 million mostly male workers their jobs. In the Los Angeles, California area alone, anywhere from forty thousand to eighty thousand men employed in blue-collar unionized professions lost their jobs.[62] Although thousands of new jobs were eventually created after this recessionary period, most of them were low-paying service positions filled predominantly by women. Prior to this economic transition the work ethic of utility for men had defined manhood by character, by the inner qualities of stoicism, integrity, reliability and the ability to shoulder burdens, the ability to put others first, the desire to protect and provide and sacrifice. . . men were not only to take care of their families, but also their societies without complaint; that was, in fact, what made them men.[63]

But even before this economic transition, the cultural supports for conformity to the traditional male role had begun to weaken. As early as the 1960's fears and anxieties that accompanied the role of the Self-Made Man began to be seen as symptomatic of the type A personality, a man who was driven, hostile and competitive. According to cardiologists, the type A personality was prone to heart attacks and other related stress disorders. In a 1974 study of close to two thousand people over age eighty, no intense, driving or highly competitive executive types were found in the entire group. Research such as this lent credibility to the belief that the Self-Made American men were literally driving themselves to death.[64] The traditional breadwinner role was being besieged from other sources. Medical research had found men to be the weaker sex, and psychologists were finding them dangerously "rigid." Events from recent wars reinforced the idea that male aggressiveness was a lethal force. Outspoken individuals from the counterculture promised a richer life for those who could overcome their masculine hang-ups. Finally, the women's movement taught men that they would *have* to change. In return, the financial arrangements that had always characterized traditional relationships between the sexes would eventually be dissolved.[65] Men who postponed marriage and avoided women who were likely to be financially dependent were no longer considered deviant, as they would have been in earlier decades, but "healthy."[66]

The recently created men's liberation movement grew out of these ideological beliefs. As the traditional male sex role came under increasing scrutiny, the men's movement taught that men, as well as women, could seek liberation from restrictive sex-role stereotypes. Because few, if any, men, were able to live up to the image of the "real" man, all men would eventually come to feel like failures as men. The psychological costs of trying to live up to this unreal image would lead men into lives of isolation and despair, characterized by repressed emotion and unfulfilled dreams. Success-driven men were seen as unable to fully trust others, unable to find satisfaction in intimate contact, were unaware of what they wanted and felt, and were rigidly resistant to opening up to discovering that part of themselves.[67]

Influenced in large part by the men's liberation paradigm, new concepts of fatherhood were introduced to middle-class men of the 1970's, 1980's and the 1990's. Men, as well as women, were perceived as victims of rigid patriarchal assumptions, which prevented them from complete fulfillment as human beings.[68] Presented in all types of support groups, classes for expectant parents and in university settings the vision and the message was everywhere: the new liberated father was a nurturing man.[69] Psychologists and child development specialists added their support for this "new" fatherhood. Research at that time suggested that a positive paternal presence was correlated with children establishing solid peer friendships and later, successful heterosexual relationships. The "new" fatherhood had gained an important measure of cultural legitimacy. In the confusion surrounding changing family values, the nurturing involved father, rather than his emotionally detached and domineering predecessor from earlier periods, had become the accepted standard.[70]

Ambivalence towards the traditional male role in our society is very much in evidence today. The passage from adolescence to adulthood has evolved from a transitional moment to a whole new stage of life; whereas, the traditional markers of manhood: leaving home, getting an education, finding a partner, starting work and becoming a father are increasingly being put off to a later date. In 1960, for instance, almost 70 percent of men had reached these milestones by the age of 30. Today, less than a third of males of that age can say the same. In 400 interviews with mainly white, college-educated men, it was found that the transition into manhood is often delayed for as long as a decade, where young men spend time together in a "world where adolescent demonstrations of manhood have replaced the real thing: responsibility."[71]

In marriages today, it's become accepted that most men and women must share in income earning for the family. This pattern has been increasing in recent decades. In 1960 42% of all families were supported solely by a male householder.[72] Today, only one in five of heterosexual couples are supported solely by a male breadwinner. Two-thirds of all mothers today are either breadwinners or co-breadwinners, in contrast with just over one quarter in 1967.[73]

In increasing numbers, women with small children have also become part of the work force. In 1950 just 23 percent of married women with children under six worked for wages; by 1986 that figure had jumped to 54 percent. Researchers agree that the collapse of fathers' capacities to support their families independently is crucial to explaining the movement of mothers into the labor force.[74]

Since the mid-1960's through to the 1980's men's income has stagnated or declined. Because fewer men could support a family on their wages alone, fewer men married at younger ages. The decreased ability to support families has been associated with a decrease in the marriage rates of young men, as well as a similar decrease in these rates for young women.[75]

There has been an increase in single-parent households. Statistics from the 2000 census shows that the number of families headed by single mothers in the United States has increased 25 percent since 1990. Demographers now predict that more than half of the children born in the last decade will spend at least part of their childhood in a single-parent home. For unmarried mothers the median age is the late

20's, and white women comprise the fastest growing segment of this group. The number of households headed by single fathers has also increased. In 2000 they headed just over 2 million households.[76]

An integral part of the cultural and economic changes over the past three decades has been the use of the no-fault concept in divorce settlements. Since women were more likely to be the plaintiffs in these proceedings, perceiving the husband as a "guilty" party often affected the size the awards that he was ordered to pay. Influenced by the no-fault concept, judges no longer viewed the non-working wife as an "aggrieved" spouse. In addition, attorneys for husbands requested that less weight be given to the areas such as the accustomed standard of living of the wife and numbers of years she had spent out of the work force. After a period of time the burden of proof shifted to the wife to show that she could not find a job.[77]

In the no-fault system a mother's unpaid work no longer automatically entitled her to ownership of any of the primary breadwinner's income, whether during marriage or after a divorce. As a result, the wife and mother who remained at home while married (as well as any children who are awarded custody to her), was almost always worse off financially after a divorce than her husband, who was able to devote his full time energies to a career.[78] Although judges continue to see women as primarily responsible for their children after divorce, support awards have tended to decrease during the same years that divorces and prices have increased.[79]

Even though our society originally never intended women to be independent persons, much less breadwinners, women have had to become increasingly dependent on their own resources. Despite impediments such as glass ceilings, sexism in the workplace and unequal pay rates for women relative to men, women have become increasingly visible in the traditional male professions of medicine, law, journalism and academia and politics.

Occurring rapidly in recent decades, these changes are shattering traditional gender conventions. Initially overcoming a number of instances of sex discrimination, Patricia Galloway has successfully worked as a civil engineer for several years.[80] Physician Zoe Buyske is one of a small group of accomplished women surgeons which have been steadily growing.[81] First becoming an Associate Justice of the State Supreme Court of South Carolina in 1988, Chief Justice Jean Hoefer Toal was elected to take the place of the retiring Chief Justice in 2000. In 2004, she was re-elected to another ten year term.[82]

Although traditionally permitted by the military to take on only "supporting" combat roles, in the conflicts in Iraq and Afghanistan, those roles involved everything from piloting combat helicopters to accompanying infantrymen and Marines on house-to-house raids. Even if working as clerks and cooks, women were still vulnerable to rocket and mortar attacks by militants.[83] Although women, who made up 15 percent of active duty personnel, earned Bronze Stars and Air Medals and were buried at Arlington and West Point, they were restricted by obsolete military traditions and regulations.[84] The military tide has recently changed for women, however. In 2012 the Marine Corps and the Army allowed women to take part in combat positions in limited arenas, and in 2013 the Secretary of Defense granted them full rights to take part in combat.

Feminism has not only changed women and how they've seen themselves. It has also changed men. Although remarkably understated and barely acknowledged publicly, in the past four decades men have had to confront challenges as radical and potentially shattering as any faced by women. As their traditional breadwinning role has eroded, many men have had to face a series of disorienting losses tied principally to the areas of status, income and privilege. Confronted with such massive changes in expectations relative to their masculine roles, many men undoubtedly have had to ask themselves, "Where do I go from here?"

Men have always proven their masculinity in a seemingly relentless series of tests, efforts that have ultimately failed to bring them closer to the self-confidence that they've sought. Many have come to understand that even if Self-Made Manhood has comprised their history, it no longer reflects their true natures. Many are learning that the manhood of the future cannot be based on obsessive self-control, defensive exclusion or frightened escape, that masculinity can be based more on the character of men's hearts and souls than on the size of their biceps or their wallets.[85]

Family and work lives have been radically altered for women. Women who work by day complain of feeling fragmented and tired as they attempt to balance the multiple responsibilities of home and family with work. Separation or divorce have forced many to confront conflicts or difficulties alone, without the help of a male partner. Although many women feel that these changes have been positive, others have suffered and continue to suffer, as they attempt to cope with new challenges for which they've had a woeful lack of training or experience. Many, however, have discovered that as frightening as it may be, overcoming new challenges can create an exciting and rewarding sense of empowerment. Although often difficult and painful, for many these changes have brought tremendous pride, joy and inner confidence. For such women it's been a price worth paying.

Tentatively, both men and women have seemed to be trying out some changes, while being unable to completely give up old beliefs and patterns. A small group of men, for instance, have assumed the role of stay at home dads, thus creating the opportunity for their wives to pursue full time careers. Although most men have learned to accept women's entrance into some traditional male preserves, many have been resistant in giving up other areas of privilege. Although in families where both couples work men have begun to assume more childcare and domestic chores, women still perform the bulk of the work associated with the "second shift." Working women often try to play the role of "superwomen" rather than expecting and demanding help from male partners with their workloads. Many women have been afraid to take on responsibilities that have been traditionally considered male preserves, such as family finances or car repair. Others have resisted the potential challenges of entering predominantly male professions, which pay more than traditional female occupations. Whereas women have few problems associating themselves with their families or communities, they often resist joining groups composed of, and working principally for, the interests of women.

If viewed from a microcosm, changes in gender relations have seemed to progress glacially, with many regressions, stops and false starts. But perceiving this period of transition globally and over the long term, these shifts have occurred at a remarkable pace, and will continue to do so as we progress forward.

Chapter 4

Gender and Codependency

He is dependent on the freshness of her emotional vitality, while she is dependent on his ability to master the world. Together they make a good team, each codependent on the other to create a whole.

> *Against the Wall*
> By Marshall Hardy,
> And John Hough

The concept of gender has been subjected to increasing scrutiny in recent years. Fraught with misunderstanding, political sensitivity and conflict, gender is one of the most problematic areas being examined today. Confusion and disagreement center about the degree to which our gender identification and accompanying behaviors are created by nature, or by nurture. As cultural constructs, masculinity and femininity are typically expressed in terms of personality traits that portray women and men as "opposite sexes." According to society's ideal, men have been depicted as aggressive, daring, rational, emotionally inexpressive, strong, cool-headed, in control of themselves, independent, active, objective, dominant, decisive, self-confident and non-nurturing. In contrast, women have been portrayed in opposite terms, such as non-aggressive, shy, intuitive, emotionally expressive, weak, hysterical, erratic and lacking in self-control, dependent, passive, subjective, submissive, indecisive, lacking in self-confidence and nurturing. As this polarity shapes how we think about stereotyped gender roles, it has often created a great divide, with men on one side and women on the other. The problem is that the concepts of femininity and masculinity don't describe most women and men as they actually are.[1] We've traditionally tended to see women and men as polar opposites, such as dominant-submissive—that don't allow for alternatives. This oppositional type of thinking puts humanity into either a dominant or a submissive, a rational or irrational camp; it implies that if you don't fit into one camp, you must fit into the other. In reality, the way that people feel and behave often depends more on the social situation they're in than it does on some rigid set of underlying traits or characteristics that defines them. A man who is assertive with his spouse may be submissive with his superior at work, or a woman who is submissive with her husband may be assertive with her children or other family members. The degree to which these individuals could be categorized as active or passive, or dominant or submissive would depend on which social context they operate from.[2]

Conceptualizing the sexes as opposites implies that women and men act in opposition to one another. It implies an underlying antagonism or conflict, the pitting of one side against the other, one way (which is right and healthy) versus the other's way (which is wrong and unhealthy). Yet nothing in the nature of women and men requires us to emphasize difference and opposition. Instead, we could emphasize similarity and reciprocity.[3]

Examining Patriarchy

The patriarchal system I knew as a child seemed benevolent and stable. Through the lens of fairy tales, legends, and stories available in the popular culture, it represented a world ruled by men who were kind, brave, fair-minded, a world where masculine values such as strength, fortitude and justice prevailed. Protective of their families, these men worked long hours to provide for them; many went to war for their loved ones and their country. From my child-like perspective the system where Dad went to work and Mom stayed home seemed perfect. The men that I knew seemed goodhearted individuals, who could be stern, but loving. They provided us with all that we needed to thrive and grow. I appreciated then and appreciate today the efforts of the men that I've known. The women I knew in those days seemed to be loving and sensitive helpmates. In the years when I grew up in the 1950's most women believed that they were achieving their true purpose in life by becoming wives and mothers. In spite of the critiques found in books such as Betty Friedan's *The Feminine Mystique*, traditional sex roles between men and women seemed largely unchanged by the time I had graduated from college in the early 1970's.

The patriarchy that we've inherited appears to have emerged as a system which enabled societies to remain in a state of perpetual "war readiness," while allowing dependent women and children a modicum of protection. In addition, it developed at a time when child mortality rates were extremely high, and, therefore, most women had to bear and raise many children. A military-like hierarchy seemed to have invaded all areas of society, even in a less formal way to the nuclear family, where the father became the family's "general," with the role of the first lieutenant falling first on his wife, and later, as they were able, to the eldest sons. The grandparents, younger women and smaller children most likely took up the rear guard, as individuals of lower status. Even though they may have played out the "general" role within their individual families, most men held places of lower status in relationship to the head patriarch of the clan, or extended family.

Ours is a system that has worked, although imperfectly, for six thousand years. As members of our society we've automatically played out our assigned roles, passed down from one generation to the next. Understanding this, why *should* we examine patriarchy? Despite its many pitfalls, this is, after all, *our* system, the one that's always taken care of us; the one that we've always known. Why should we bother to examine it? The following are several compelling reasons.

1. Patriarchy is structured as a hierarchy; consequently, relationships formed because of its influence tend to be polarized into dominant and non-dominant roles. Many of the social roles that we take part in are influenced by this top-down system. This ranked quality to a large degree influences all our relationships.

2. A patriarchal society is male-centered, male-identified and male-dominated. As a consequence, women and feminine values are subordinated to men and masculine values.[4]

3. Patriarchy contradicts one of our core values of equal opportunity for all. In a hierarchical structure less powerful individuals will always tend to be subordinated to those that are more powerful, and, as a consequence, most often perceive themselves as victims. Most individuals suffer from some feelings of inferiority because of their subordinate status in relationship to the people above them.

4. As a hierarchy, patriarchy creates codependent behavior patterns between any two dominant and non-dominant individuals. In most instances, the man is conditioned to play the dominant role in relationship to others. Nevertheless, the dominant role can be played out by women, as well. Patriarchal rules can be administered by women, who, if raised in patriarchal families, can learn to be as controlling and repressive as their male models.[5] An example of this phenomenon is described by Dave Pelzer in his book, *A Child Called "It."* In his narrative, Pelzer describes years of abusive treatment by his mother, who was the dominant individual in the family. Powerless to stop her virulent behavior, Pelzer's father, who was also the breadwinner, eventually turned his back on Dave and his brothers by walking away from the family. By doing so he handed over his remaining power to his dangerously unstable wife.

5. A patriarchal system is fear-based; it creates a fixed pattern to either dominate or be dominated. Power is often maintained through either subtle or blatant intimidation. Those who learn to play subordinate roles, and who are encouraged to perceive themselves as powerless, rarely learn to be effective advocates for

Elizabeth Ralston

either themselves or others in their care. In contrast, dominant individuals fail to develop interpersonal skills such as empathy and compassion and tend to objectify those they dominate. A devastating example of how these polarizing roles interact takes place in our schools with numbing regularly. In January 2010 at a high school in western Massachusetts a 15-year old immigrant from Ireland committed suicide by hanging after she was subjected to unrelenting bullying for three months by a group of students in her high school class. At a loss as to how to respond to the bullying, the adults involved either ignored or overlooked it, and by doing so, appeared to passively tolerate it. Because the bullying was allowed to continue, the victim could see no way out of her hopeless situation except to take her own life.

6. Patriarchy tends to be an entrenched system; it resists change and seeks to maintain its own stability. Many who perceive themselves as victims find multiple roadblocks in their ability to significantly improve their lives. This could explain why major changes in our educational, political and religious institutions have historically been difficult to achieve, and often occur only after many years of struggle.

7. Regardless of an individual's gender, the system ultimately exists for the head patriarch. The men who truly prosper under this system are in the top rungs of the power structure. Traditionally, masculine hierarchies exclude not only women but also most men. Male elites are as interested in exercising sway over other men in the same organization as they are in defending the organization as a whole.[6] Because

the system exists primarily for those on the top, the extent of suffering of those on the bottom often tends to be either minimized or denied by those in the power elite.

Patriarchal systems have certain rules in common. Some of the most damaging are:

a) Blind obedience. Patriarchy stands upon this foundation. The act of obeying in itself is considered virtuous, and one of the rules is never to question the rules.

b) The repression of all emotions except fear. The emotion of anger is considered especially dangerous to the patriarchal system. The loss of our ability to be angry encourages us to become weak-willed and people pleasers. Individuals can become so nice that they are unable to fight for the causes that they believe in.

c) The repression of individual willpower. Willful and energetic individuals are hard for patriarchy to control. The individual is left with two choices: conforming or rebelling.

d) The repression of thinking if it departs from the way of thinking of the authority figure. Although advancements have been made in political democracies, the systems in place in the family, some religious, educational and employment settings remain rigidly patriarchal.[7]

Another important factor in maintaining our dominant culture is to deny its negative aspects. Doing this enables us to participate within its structure, automatically, without thinking or evaluating the actions of ourselves or others.

As members of a society, we find it difficult or impossible to acknowledge the roots of patriarchy and our involvement in it. We resist even saying the word "patriarchy" in polite conversation. We act as if patriarchy wasn't there, because the realization that it does exist is like a door that swings in only one direction. Once through, we can't go back again to not knowing. We cling to the illusion that everything is basically all right, . . .and that if we only leave things alone, they'll stay pretty much as they are and, we often like to think, always have been.[8]

Even though it's tempting to assign blame for our system, no one group can be blamed for it. Although none of us created it, we have all helped to perpetuate it, and we all share in its inheritance. Systems aren't able to do or feel any thing and therefore can't be held to account as people can. Therefore, directing blame and guilt against groups or individuals treats as psychological and individualistic something that's a *systemic* problem.[9] The choice for individuals is about how to participate in this system differently so that we can help to change not only ourselves, but the world that shapes our lives. . . Ultimately, the choice is about empowering ourselves to take our share of responsibility for the social institution that we've inherited.[10]

A critique of our social system and how it structures relations between the genders is not a presumption of change for the parts of it that are healthy and working well. It is important, however, to critically examine those areas which appear to limit or restrict the mental, emotional and spiritual growth of men and women in order to ascertain healthier ways that individuals can relate to themselves as well as to to others.

Cultural Mythology

Legends, myths and stories reflect our understanding of the past and reinforce our expectations for the future. The stories transmitted to us by movies, television, books and magazine articles have, to a large degree, taken on the role traditionally played by the legends and myths of our past. In doing so, they transmit our society's expectations to us with images that are at times endemic and pervasive, at others, subtle and understated. These images have become so embedded in our cultural landscape that at times we are unable to even recognize them or acknowledge their influence in our lives. Nevertheless, their effect on our awareness of ourselves as well as our relationship to others is deep and profound. It's important to examine how messages from our popular culture influence our perceptions of gender roles.

A cursory review of story lines currently viewed on television and in the movies is illustrative. Men figure prominently as heroes and villains. Although women can play these roles, as well, they are much more likely to be portrayed as victims than are men. Action in movies has typically surrounded a central male character or characters who are surrounded by lesser men and women, who play ancillary roles in relationship to these central characters. In a review of recent movies, such as *The Bourne Identity*, *Iron Man, Rambo* and *I am Legend*, as well as past cinematic offerings such as *Star Wars* and the *James Bond* series, the action is defined by men and by male heroic values. Even if in a starring role, the women are generally in a supportive capacity in relationship to the leading male. For example, in the Broadway play, *The Producers,* the main action is played by two strong male leading actors. The main female part is that of a young Swedish actress, whose primary purpose is merely to provide romantic interest and comic relief.

In musicals and/or movies such as *Carousel*, *Sweet Charity*, and *The Purple Rose of Cairo* women have often been portrayed as helpless victims, who, for the most part, are dominated by the men around them. The theme of female helplessness is most blatant in the 1930's classic movie, *King Kong*. Kidnapped by a giant gorilla, the female protagonist, a helpless "weak" woman, struggles, crying and screaming, throughout most of the movie, while she is repeatedly rescued from the monster's clutches by the "strong" leading man. In movies such as *The Three Faces of Eve* and more recently, in movies such as *Girl Interrupted* and *The Black Swan*, women have been portrayed as psychologically handicapped or mentally unstable. Movies such as *Elizabeth, Steele Magnolias, Places in the Heart, Norma Rae* and *The Help*, which portray strong and enduring women, are less common than the male-dominated action themes found in movies today.

Over the past few years women have begun to be portrayed increasingly as protagonists in partnerships with men, as they've solved crimes as police officers, doctors, lawyers or judges on prime time T. V. shows; they've occasionally played political leaders in such series as *Commander in Chief* and *Political Animals*. Movies such as *Brave, Frozen* and *Hunger Games* have featured young women as protagonists. Although certainly welcomed, these plot-line changes have been fairly recent.

Boys and young men have grown up with a stream of images fed by the media of men as "heroes" who save those weaker than themselves. Some of the ideas transmitted from these images to young men are that men can trust themselves, take risks, and take action in ways that are courageous and valuable to society. In contrast, because our media has created images for women that have encouraged them more often to play "victim" than "heroine" roles, they've often transmitted messages to women that have led them to believe that they are unable to trust or take care of themselves, that they are not as important or as competent as men and that they live in a dangerous, fearful world. The result of these contrasting messages is to maintain a status quo where men remain dominant and women submissive.

Carol Tavris has conjectured about the dilemma of women and the effect on them of the messages they receive:

> And the classic woman's story, whether in ancient fairy tales like "Cinderella" and "Sleeping Beauty" or their modern equivalents in romance novels and films like *Pretty Woman*, is a narrative of passivity, chance, and fate. Horrible things, all of them beyond her control, happen to the beautiful heroine who awaits rescue by her Prince. Until he saves her, she is doomed to a life of sweeping, cleaning, struggling, prostitution, or corporate executive hood. If she isn't beautiful, pliant, and willing to give it all up for love, she doesn't get rescued. What effect does this story, endlessly repeated throughout our culture, have on women's identities and dreams?[11]

Examining Gender Roles

Psychologist John Gray, in his extremely popular 1992 book *Men are From Mars, Women are from Venus,* characterized men and women based on traditional gender roles from earlier decades. In describing men, for instance, Gray used terms such as power, competency, efficiency and achievement; he depicted men as continually trying to develop their power and skills, with a sense of self defined through their ability to accomplish results. According to Gray, men are more interested in "objects" and "things" than in people and feelings.[12] Conversely, according to Gray, women value love, communication, beauty and relationships. They spend a lot of time supporting and helping one another; their sense of self is defined through their feelings and the quality of their relationships. They experience fulfillment through sharing and relating, and are primarily relationship, rather than goal oriented.[13] Although Gray attempted to describe gender relations in an even-handed and objective way, he failed to address the root causes of gender stereotypes. Doing so would have allowed him to at least partially answer the question of *why* men and women act as though they've been raised on different planets.

In her book *Necessary Dreams* Dr. Anna Fels addresses some of these questions by describing how the traditional visions of the future for men and women parted ways mainly in the public arena. For men, work outside the home was not only a financial necessity, it was central to his identity and self-worth. Women, on the other hand, were defined by their role. . . as an adjunct to and provider for others within the private sphere. Private relationships represented women's sole source of identity and affirmation. Consequently, they carefully developed the skills required to maximize their narrowly defined opportunities. For women, a huge premium was placed on physical attractiveness, sensitivity and service to others.[14]

During the latter part of the nineteenth century, into the early part of the twentieth century a few women were able to experience the first part of ambition, to achieve success in the public realm and to develop areas of expertise outside of the domestic sphere. Openly working toward, and taking pleasure in, the recognition of their achievements, however, remained off-limits. Today, while more women are able to succeed in the public sphere, there are still unspoken injunctions about women achieving because of personal ambition. The story of former Speaker of the House Nancy Pelosi is a good example. The narrative of her rise to congresswoman contains no reference to her own aspirations to achieving personal power. Pelosi transitioned from a behind-the scenes party functionary to a front-line politician because of a promise she had made to a dying friend. Once in Congress, although she admitted loving the job, she added that she never craved it.[15]

The most famous and widely used psychological measure of femininity, masculinity and androgyny is an instrument called the revised Bem Sex Role Inventory (BSRI). The BSRI is . . . considered one of the standard measures in psychology. The following are the twenty traits chosen to define femininity in the BSRI: *yielding, loyal, cheerful, compassionate, shy, sympathetic, affectionate, sensitive to the needs of others, flatterable, understanding, eager to soothe hurt feelings, soft-spoken, warm, tender, gullible, childlike, does not use harsh language, loves children, gentle.*[16] A close analysis of these seemingly harmless adjectives is revealing: the woman they describe is socially recessive, exquisitely responsible to others' feelings and undemanding about getting her own needs for affirmation met. As one analyzes the BSRI adjectives, two basic elements of femininity emerge. The first is that femininity can only exist within the context of a relationship. By definition one can be yielding, affectionate, or sensitive only in relation to someone else. The second element of femininity that emerges from the BSRI is that a woman must be providing something for the other person in the relationship, be that person a lover, a child, a sick parent, a husband, or even a boss. Giving to and providing for the needs of others is the core emotional activity that defines femininity.[17]

Elizabeth Ralston

Masculinity, by contrast, is defined neither by relationships, nor by providing for others. In fact, it is defined by the opposite. The BSRI adjectives that describe masculinity are: *self-reliant, strong personality, forceful, independent, analytical, defines one's beliefs, athletic, assertive, has leadership abilities, willing to take risks, makes decisions easily, self-sufficient, dominant, willing to take a stand, aggressive, acts as a leader, individualistic, competitive, ambitious.* . . Not only can you be solitary and masculine, but if you are in a relationship that involves overt dependency or being influenced by others (which almost all relationships do), as a man, your masculine sexual identity is at risk.[18]

I.K. Broverman's classic study on the perception of gender shows that in our culture a healthy male and a healthy adult are perceived as one and the same. Participants in her study had a negative view of femininity which implied that it's not possible to be both feminine and adult at the same time. In the study male and female participants checked off adjectives describing healthy men, healthy women and healthy adults. The results indicated that participants described healthy men and healthy adults as having the same qualities, whereas they described healthy women as having quite different qualities than healthy adults. For example, healthy women were described as passive, dependent and illogical, while healthy adults were described as active, independent and logical. It proved impossible to score as a healthy adult and a healthy woman.[19]

In her book *Toward a New Psychology of Women,* Jean Baker Miller states that in psychotherapy, women often spend a great deal more time talking about giving than men do. Women constantly confront themselves with questions about giving. Am I giving enough? Can I give enough? Why don't I give enough? . . . They are upset if they feel they are not givers. By contrast, the question of whether he is a giver or giving enough does not enter into a man's self-image. Few men feel that it is a primary issue in their struggle for identity. They are concerned much more about "doing." Am I a doer? Do I measure up to the proper image of someone who does?[20]

Traditionally, the reference point for men, the point around which their lives revolve—is located within themselves, the part of their psyche in psychological terms is named the ego ideal. Men seek to live up to the standards of this ideal self, the part of them which require them to achieve higher positions, earn more money and make new sexual conquests. In contrast, for women raised in the traditional female model, the center of gravity does not lie within the self. It rather lies between themselves and other people. Women often measure their value in terms of the quality of their transactions with others.[21]

Gray concurs; he describes a women's sense of self to be defined primarily by her feelings and by the quality of her relationships. He perceives women to be happy simply when they understand that their needs will be met.[22] Conversely, men are happy by being competent, autonomous, and by independently solving problems.[23]

Gray leaves few options for a woman who wants to express her wants and needs to a man; he states that when she criticizes or tries to improve him, the man can feel controlled, mistrusted or rejected. In his opinion the main job of a woman is to accept a man unconditionally, exactly as he is, and that once he feels accepted, he will grow on his own.[24] In advising women that they must play only a passive role in relation to their male partners, Gray implies that women have few rights to speak directly to men regarding problems they may be having. Although he encourages men to listen to women express their feelings, his description of men and women suggests that women do not have the same needs as men in areas such as feeling competent and being accepted unconditionally.[25] His assumptions about men's and women's differences lead us to believe that women have few needs in the area of competency, and that men have few needs in the area of relationships. Gray's description of men and women from different planets obscures the fact that in reality we have all come from the same planet, in most cases have attended the same or similar educational institutions, and have been exposed to similar messages about the importance of achievement, competency and relationships.

Trained to feel comfortable in the world of things and abstract ideas, a traditional male may have little empathetic connection to others, little emotional relatedness to his own family, little attunement to his own internal world and little willingness or capacity to "hang in" when a relationship develops conflicts. Many men under-function in the area of emotional relatedness, and their under-functioning is closely related to a women's over-functioning in this area. It is therefore not surprising when a "hysterical," over-emotional female ends up under the same roof as the unemotional, distant male.[26]

For a traditional male, masculinity is defined by a core need to control. A real man has to be in control or at least give the impression of being in control. The more men see control as central to their sense of self, well-being, worth and safety, the more driven they feel to go after it and to organize their lives around it. The more men participate in the system, the more they come to see themselves as separate, autonomous and disconnected from others. The practice of control is a core principle of social life that defines manhood.[27]

The principal motivation in subscribing to these ideals is not because men want to impress women, or to meet an abstract standard. They do it because men want to be positively evaluated by other men. Men often hear the voices of the men in their lives—their fathers, coaches, brothers, grandfathers, uncles, priests—to inform their ideas of masculinity.[28]

Attempts to categorize males and females into rigid gender-based roles are extremely limiting to each gender. Elaborate differences are often created where none exist. . . Yet, despite of all these pervasive efforts to categorize and limit, the little boy who is ridiculed for crying "like a girl" doesn't stop feeling sad, he just buries that emotion; and the little girl who is punished for willfulness as a "tomboy" just takes that spirit underground. Later, since both have been told that some part of themselves is appropriate only to the "opposite sex," they will look for that part of themselves in other people. In search of inner wholeness, they will try to absorb and possess someone else. . . . [29]

> This polarization of "feminine" and "masculine" would be cruel enough if its effects went no further, but the two halves aren't really "halves" at all. Male dominance means that admired qualities are called "masculine" and are more plentiful, while "feminine" ones are not only fewer but also less valued. Thus, boys as a group have higher self-esteem because they are literally allowed more of a self and because the qualities they must suppress are less desirable, while girls as a group have lower self-esteem because they are expected to suppress more of themselves and because society denigrates what is left.[30]

Carol Tavris has cited new studies that show that the stereotyped behavior that we link to gender is not necessarily tied to an individual's biological sex. Sometimes this behavior is linked to what an individual is doing or needs to do. For example, in a study by sociologist Barbara Risman, having responsibility for childcare was as strongly related to "feminine" traits such as nurturance and sympathy, as being female was. She reported that single men who cared for children behaved more like mothers than like married fathers. In a study of 150 men who were spending up to sixty hours a week caring for their ailing parents, the director of the research reported that the men spent as much time as women doing nurturing things such as holding the sick relative's hands, listening and showing concern.[31] Other researchers have found that although both men and women *think* that women have the empathetic advantage over men, research indicates that there are no real gender differences in the ability to be empathetic. Although men and women may be helpful in different ways, the impetus to help is also present in both genders.[32]

Tavris continues challenging gender stereotypes by pointing out that, although women have traditionally been considered peace-loving nurturers, they have historically supported the efforts of their countries in times of war. She notes that by supporting polarizing sexual stereotypes such as those of men as warlike and women as peace makers and life creators, we fail to notice women who support and endorse war, or men who promote pacifism and cooperative values. She adds that these stereotypes are inaccurate blue prints of the activities and potentials of both men and women.[33]

Gender and Learning Potential

Although sex differences in tests scores persist, we still can make one statement with confidence: the range of performance within each sex far exceeds the differences between the sexes. Researchers Jacklin and Maccoby assert that . . .publications concentrate not on whether a sex difference exists but on how large a difference really exists. These analyses are sobering if we consider the social implications of the work. It is completely impossible to predict an individual's abilities on the basis of his or her sex. Large numbers of both sexes score at the high end of the distribution for all cognitive tests—enough to fill society's need for persons of exceptional skill.[34]

Arguments persist as to whether or not gender differences are inherent or due to environmental factors. It's absurd to conclude that the differences in aptitude in different areas between men and women are primarily because of biology or environment. The two interact from the time of conception.[35] Furthermore, although men's brains are slightly larger than women's brains, brain size does not predict intellectual performance as was once thought. Men and women perform similarly in IQ tests. In addition, most scientists still cannot tell male from female brains just by looking at them.[36]

Despite stereotyped dogma regarding inherent male versus female abilities in areas such as mathematics, recent studies suggest that where differences exist, nurture, rather than nature is responsible. Although in 1983, the Study of Mathematically Precocious Youth found a 13 to 1 boy-girl imbalance of children younger than 13 who scored 700 or better on the mathematics portion of the SAT, by 2005 that statistic had fallen to 2.8 to 1. Nothing in the brain that is "hard wired" can change that quickly (i.e., over a twenty-two year period). Cross-cultural data on young people with exceptional mathematical ability is even more telling. Top scorers in the International Mathematical Olympiad, a nine hour, six problem exam, demonstrated a pattern of dominant participation by foreign-born girls. Whereas countries such as Bulgaria, East Germany, and U.S.S.R/Russia included 21, 19 and 15 girls, respectively, the U. S. team included only three. Since 1988, Bulgarian girls have won twice as many medals in the International Olympiad as American girls. Even in neighboring countries with a common gene pool, such as the former East Germany and West Germany and Slovakia and the Czech Republic, the first of each pair regularly send many more girls to the Olympiad by margins of 18 to 0 and 22 to 10, respectively. It's hard to see that as anything but the result of the starkly different social and other environmental forces in each country, and not intrinsic biology.[37]

In Iceland, gender stereotypes have been further challenged as boys in this northern country trail far behind girls by an average of 15 points in mathematical achievement on a standardized test designed by the Organization of Economic Cooperation and Development. In remote Icelandic fishing villages, such as Sandgerdi on the southwestern end of the country, the difference in mathematical achievement between girls and boys is closer to 30 points on this standardized test. Many boys in these villages have reported feeling bored by school, wanting to leave school early to become fishermen like their fathers. The high achieving girls, by contrast, perceive achievement in mathematics as a means to achieve the skills necessary to leave their isolated villages for more urban areas.[38]

Lise Eliot, a neuroscientist at Rosalind Franklin University of Medicine and Science refutes assertions of significant differences in male and female brains. In a rigorous review of the research, she notes that a study which indicates the band of fibers connecting the right and left brain is larger in women, thus creating their ability for more holistic thinking, is based on a single 1982 study of only 14 brains. Fifty other studies, taken together, found no such sex difference in either infants or adults. Eliot points out that some differences in behaviors of boy and girl babies can be created by parental expectations. Dozens of disguised gender experiments have shown that adults perceive baby boys and girls differently, seeing the same behavior through gender-tinted lenses. How we perceive children. . .shapes how we treat them and therefore what experiences we give them. Since life experiences can form the very structure and function of the brain, these various experiences produce sex differences in adult behavior and brains – the result not of innate and inborn nature, but of nurture. Eliot points out, for example, that children settle into sex-based play preferences only around the age of one, which is when they grasp which sex they are and strongly identify with it. Prior to this, a host of studies point out that infants of both sexes prefer dolls to trucks. By the time they're in pre-school, children's sex-identification produce preferences which snowball, producing brains with different talents.[39]

Experts disagree as to the degree that testosterone creates aggression in males. A review of scientific studies of preadolescent and early adolescent boys, however, concludes that there is no evidence of an association between testosterone and aggressive behavior.[40] The typical action of a hormone is to change over time in response to environmental events, and testosterone is no different. In many cases where high levels of testosterone are measured, they are the *effect* of aggression rather than the cause of it. Anthropological studies of peaceful societies such as the Semoi of Malaysia, the Hutterite Brethren or the Amish of North America prove that peaceful, non-violent societies can exist successfully.[41]

Elizabeth Ralston

Gender Relations in the Dysfunctional Family

In its traditional form, patriarchy works best when those who take part in it believe that it's a fair and equitable system. Within its structure, we negotiate and make compromises. In the realm of marriage and family, we accommodate and learn to accept what we assume will be equitable trade-offs. If someone sacrifices in one area, they expect to be paid back in another. The woman who sacrifices her career for marriage and family, for instance, will expect that her husband will take care of her and her children financially.

It is most often in families where addiction is present that this system of accommodation begins to break down. Relationships with addicted individuals can become one-sided affairs, with the bulk of the responsibilities being shouldered by the non-addicted spouse or partner. Under the influence of alcohol or drugs, the addicted spouse may be physically and/ or verbally abusive, behave irresponsibly with the family's finances or may abandon the family altogether. The non-addicted spouse often becomes an enabler and a caretaker, taking over neglected areas of the alcoholic or addict's life. It was during counseling sessions with non-addicted spouses of alcoholics and addicts that the term codependency was first coined. It is noteworthy that most of the non-addicted spouses first labeled as codependent were women.[42]

The possibility that cultural conditioning may contribute to codependency has only recently been addressed. As the traditional female role is an almost totally codependent one, it's not surprising that many more women than men report codependent behavior patterns. The role copies the definition of codependency as one who has the need to please, care for and otherwise help others at the expense of adequately caring for herself. As a result of this clinical definition, women, and their ability to sacrifice themselves on behalf of others have at times been labeled as pathological. Finding themselves labeled as codependent, these women can be blamed for being excessively feminine. According to psychologists Marshall Hardy and John Hough, separating the parental culture's rules on gender from our understanding of codependency is the only way to avoid this needless and sexist creation of a pathological feminine state.[43]

In her essay, "Codependency and the Myth of Recovery, a Feminist Scrutiny," Kay Hagan believes that codependency illustrates a pattern of dominance and subordination in intimate relationships. Hagan summarizes the primary characteristics of subordinate codependency as follows: External referencing, characterized by always checking outside of myself before making choices, martyrdom, characterized by taking care of others while sacrificing one's own needs, poor self-esteem, characterized by feeling less than, unworthy, undeserving, controlling behavior, characterized by obsessing over one's partner's behavior or manipulation, demoralization: feeling hopeless, despairing, victimized, and deriving a feeling of self-worth from being needed. A subordinate individual in a dominant/subordinate system learns this behavior pattern early in life and can become very creative at fulfilling others' needs. Subordinates can forget that they have needs; in fact, their lives are easier if they don't have needs.[44]

As mentioned earlier, a core value for a man is to be "in charge" and "in control;" a man initiates this process by being "in control" of himself and his own emotions. By extension, men often feel the need to "manage" or exert control over others, a behavior which often provokes resentments,

Elizabeth Ralston

alienation, and withdrawal behaviors in others. The need to control serves to reinforce the emotional isolation of the controller. As a consequence, because of their attitude and accompanying behaviors, many men become psychologically divorced from those they really care about. This need severely limits the range of feelings that men feel they can safely express. It's telling that one of the basic conditions of codependency is also an intrinsic part of the male code: *Don't talk, don't feel, don't express.*[45]

Psychologists Hardy and Hough define the two types of codependency which mirror the male and female stereotypes. The masculine version of codependency, which they label Type I, is characterized by adjectives such as selfish, powerful, self-centered, isolated, invulnerable, strong, independent, insensitive and unexpressive. In contrast, the feminine version of codependency, or Type II, is characterized by adjectives such as pleasing, powerless, selfless, no anger, enmeshed, too vulnerable, weak, dependent, overly sensitive and overly expressive.[46]

Case Histories

For the purposes of this book, I use the term "dominant" to describe the stereotypically masculine pattern of behavior which can lead to an overt and direct controlling pattern of codependency and the term "non-dominant" to describe the stereotypical female version of behavior, which can lead to a more passive, indirect controlling pattern of codependency. Although not all men will conform to the masculine stereotype, nor will all women conform to the feminine, because of their respective gender conditioning, more women will tend to demonstrate more of the non-dominant characteristics, and more men will tend to demonstrate more of the dominant characteristics. Regardless of his or her gender, however, most codependents' behaviors lie somewhere along the dominant/non-dominant continuum. For example, an individual might exhibit a blend of both dominant and non-dominant behavior patterns, showing dominant behavior in one or more social situations, and non-dominant in others. The following case histories will illustrate some similarities and differences in codependent behaviors in a small group of women and men.

The middle sister of four siblings, Mary was raised to be a good and obedient daughter. As she grew up, she found that care-taking was her primary way of gaining attention. Raised in a conservative Christian community, she was encouraged to play this role. While in school she took care of her maiden aunt and would regularly do favors for her siblings. Nevertheless, she had a very distant relationship to her parents, especially with her father. Growing up, Mary had trouble making decisions because she had never developed a good understanding of her likes and dislikes. She was dependent on her husband and other strong-minded individuals in her family for decision-making. After she raised her family, she became the family caretaker, caring for the elderly and ill in her family, including her husband. She received no help with these responsibilities. Mary suffered for many years from low self esteem and depression and sought treatment in mental health settings; her behavior has most closely resembled the non-dominant pattern of codependency.

John often felt shy and awkward as a boy. His father was a domineering, critical man who would often fly into rages. He rarely talked back to his father and used his mother, who tended to be passive and non-dominant, as a role model. By the time he had reached adolescence, John knew that he was gay. In high school he felt like a misfit and was often bullied by aggressive male students. After graduating from college, he suffered from chronic feelings of low self-esteem and anxiety. He had difficulty in asking for his needs to be met from others. As he matured, John became involved in the Adult Children of Alcoholics' twelve step recovery program. He also became involved in individual counseling and in men's groups. He sought to involve himself in activities which have helped him enhance his self-esteem and sense of empowerment. John has admitted that he still has problems asserting himself with others and asking for his needs to be met. John's behavior is most similar to the non-dominant pattern of codependency.

Although Joe had a successful in his career as a police officer, his wife of twenty years had recently left him. She reported that he would often lose his temper and fly into rages, which created a home environment ruled by fear and intimation. She was afraid to be around him because she feared for her physical safety. Joe was unaware of his domineering and abusive behavior and thought that he had been behaving "normally" all these years. Wanting to gain more insight into his own behavior, Joe checked himself into a treatment program for codependency. Joe realized that his tendency to rage and to lose his temper come from examples of and in reaction to treatment from his abusive, alcoholic father. Working with a therapist he had come to trust, he has discovered many instances where his suppressed feelings of fear, pain and grief helped to create his obsessive need to control members of his family. Joe's behavior most closely resembles the dominant pattern of codependency.

The oldest of four siblings, Stephanie became a "little mother" in helping her mother to care for her younger siblings. Stephanie's father was a corporate executive, and her mother, an elementary school teacher. Both of her parents gave her messages that she could achieve anything that she set out to do. Although Stephanie's father had a dominant personality, and was a harsh taskmaster, as she grew older, she adopted him as a role model. As a child she learned to dominate her younger siblings and neighborhood friends. She assumed leadership roles at school. After graduating from college, Stephanie married and started a family. Several years later, Stephanie obtained a management position in a large company. Considered an effective manager at work, her dominant style nevertheless began to adversely affect her personal relationships with family and friends. After Stephanie's son developed a bed-wetting problem, she sought help from a family therapist, who eventually referred her to Co-Dependents' Anonymous. In recovery, she began to realize that her dominant style may have helped to create her son's problems, as well as to alienate her from family and friends. Stephanie's behavior has most closely resembled the dominant style of codependency.

The inner realities of dominant and non-dominant individuals may paradoxically be very similar. A dominant individual's need to shame others may stem from his/her deep-seated fear of being shameful, whereas a non-dominant's fear of losing another's approval may be caused by a similar fear of being shamed. Observable behaviors labeled as "strong" or "weak" can effectively mask an individual's true feelings, as both may have similar experiences of fear, loss, shame and abandonment, numbness, denial, confusion and rigidity. The polarized behaviors of both can reveal similar

Elizabeth Ralston

emotional sources.[47] In his book *Healing the Shame Within*, John Bradshaw describes the similarities of two individuals who appear to be opposites. Each may cover up in ways that appear opposite in nature, but each is still driven by neurotic shame. In fact, the most paradoxical aspect of neurotic shame is that it is the core motivator of the super-achiever and the under-achiever, the Star and the Scapegoat, the "Righteous" and the wretched, the powerful and the pathetic.[48]

Suzanne is passive when interacting with her domineering husband; however, she is appropriately assertive when dealing with her children. Sean is quiet and compliant while at work, although he is controlling and dominant while at home with his wife. Many codependents exhibit a combination of dominant and non-dominant behaviors.

Women often demonstrate a combination of these opposite behaviors. A successful executive who was assertive with others both in work and non-work settings, Rachel joined Codependents Anonymous because of conflicts that she experienced in raising her daughter. She and her husband disagreed about appropriate ways to raise their daughter, however, especially in the area of limit-setting. When Rachel would set what she thought was an appropriate limit, her husband would contradict her in front of their daughter. This pattern would place her in the role of the "bad" mother in the eyes of her daughter and would make Rachel feel helpless in setting any limits at all with her daughter. Although Rachel played the role of the non-dominant codependent with her family, overall, her behavior demonstrates a mixture of both dominant and non-dominant patterns.

Men can demonstrate a mixture of dominant and non-dominant behaviors, as well. Raised in a rough neighborhood, as a young man, at times Ed had to adopt hyper-masculine dominant behaviors just to survive. Years later, however, he found himself playing the role of the caretaker with family members, all of whom were addicted. He has had relationships with women where he has played both dominant and non-dominant roles. Ed has been attending twelve-step recovery programs for several years. Throughout this time period, he has shown a mixture of dominant and non-dominant codependent behavior patterns.

Regardless of whether a man or a woman manifests the codependent behavior most characteristic of his or her gender, it is critical that he or she address the issue of gender conditioning at some point during the recovery process. Taking this action is crucial, since as a society we tend to minimize or deny the degree to which gender relations affect us. To ignore this part of our lives is to overlook an imposing mass of information regarding our personal histories that enables us to perceive ourselves as members of a larger society. Omitting or minimizing this conditioning is to leave the recovery process, as well as our knowledge of it, only partially defined, shallow and distorted, not unlike the experience of a proverbial "fish out of water." Treating codependency solely as an individual problem can cause individuals to inaccurately perceive themselves as if they have been living muffled, in a vacuum, permanently detached from their communities and culture.

A better understanding of one's gender conditioning could clarify why it may be difficult for an individual to change certain behaviors. As an example, a woman in recovery who's had problems letting go of her obsession to please others may find it helpful to take a closer look at expectations that may have been placed on her to play out a traditional female role throughout her life. By contrast, a man who's had difficulties in expressing his feelings in group settings may find the origin of his problem may lie in his conditioning as a man which has encouraged him hide his emotions from others. Whether an individual is involved in a twelve-step recovery program, or whether he or she is simply interested in gaining insight of a personal nature, the dynamics of gender conditioning can add an invaluable and vital dimension to one's evolving journey of self-discovery.

Chapter 5

Women and Codependency

I had gone into marriage and parenthood with the misconception that if I gave all of me to my husband and children, I would truly have given my family all that I could. Unfortunately, I gave away so much of me that there was nothing left. I no longer had an identity. I no longer had laughter and spontaneity. I lived in fear and terror. I was as good as a dead person.

"Beth's Story"
From Co-Dependents Anonymous

Pre-adolescence

Pre-adolescent girls, from ages 7 to roughly 12 years of age, are interested in everything—sports, nature, people, music and books. They bake pies, solve mysteries, act like tomboys and are confident that they can take care of themselves. They have the ability to perform competently in any situation, regardless of the expectations of gender constraints. Curious, adventurous, courageous and ambitious, they are risk-takers and will confront a myriad of challenges, such as caring for a baby, cooking a meal or changing a tire. Almost all of the heroines of girls' literature are from this age group. Because of their healthy outlook, young girls from this age group rarely need to come into therapy.[1]

Adolescence

In the next stage of development, however, life can take a different turn for girls. According to psychoanalyst Erick Erickson the stage of adolescence describes the autonomous, initiating, industrious self through the forging of an identity that can support and justify adult commitments. Unfortunately, when Erickson wrote about this stage of development, he, along with other child development theorists of his era, was referring only to the male adolescent. From Erickson's perspective, the female adolescent's identity to a large degree would remain in a diffuse, suspended state, as she prepared to attract the man by whose name she would be known and by whose status she would be defined. In addition to defining her existence, the man would rescue her from an otherwise lonely and empty life by filling her "inner space."

Whereas for the male child, identity and intimacy are two separate stages of development, for the female child, these tasks seem to be fused into one. From Erickson's perspective intimacy is connected to identity as the female comes to know herself primarily through her relationships with others.[2]

According to psychoanalyst Bruno Bettelheim, the female adolescent experiences a period of intense passivity and submissiveness in which nothing overtly happens to her. In the deep sleeps of the fairy-tale princesses Snow White and Sleeping Beauty, Bettelheim describes an inner concentration in the young female, which he considers to be the necessary counterpart to the male's need for activity and adventure. When the heroine awakens, her destiny is to marry the prince, and not to slay a dragon or conquer a mythical monster, as does the male.[3]

In her book *Reviving Ophelia,* Mary Piper describes the transition that young girls make from pre-adolescence into adolescence: In early adolescence, studies show that girls' IQ scores drop, and their math and science scores plummet. They lose their resiliency and optimism and become less curious and inclined to take risks. Formerly tomboys, they lose their assertive, energetic personalities and become more deferential, self-critical and depressed. They report unhappiness with their own bodies. Piper continues: Girls become "female impersonators" who fit their whole selves into small, crowded spaces. Vibrant, self-confident girls transition to shy, insecure teen-agers. These girls stop thinking, "Who am I?" or "What do I want?" And start thinking, "What must I do to please others?"[4]

In her book, *The Curse of the Good Girl*, Rachel Simmons describes the feminine ethic, the product of a culture which remains confused about gender equality. This ethic urges girls to be perfect and selfless. This role model not only creates a troubled relationship for girls in the areas of personal integrity and failure, but it demands modesty, depriving girls of permission to commit to their strengths and goals. This stereotyped pattern causes diminished assertive body language, quiets voices and weakens handshakes in girls; the "curse" cuts to the core of authentic selfhood, demanding that girls curb the strongest feelings and desires that form, in Simmons' words, a "patchwork" of a person.[5] According to Simmons the need to be "good" is a fundamentally self-limiting experience: the need to be "perfect" and "do everything right" leaves many girls uncomfortable with feedback and failure. . .The need to be nice or right at all costs leaves these girls on the sidelines as they avoid the situations that aren't sure things: moments of self-assertion that require healthy risk-taking, and which might lead to failure, disappointment or another person's unhappiness.[6]

The rules that require young women to self-promote, negotiate and absorb feedback, find them ill-prepared for success in the world of work in today's world. By the first day of her first job, it's often too late, as the Good Girl habits are firmly in place.[7] Although girls understand the importance of tangible items they can put on their resumes, such as a high GPA and good work experience, there is a less obvious, but no less important inner resume we must help girls develop, a set of skills which turns a young woman from a "Good Girl" to a "Real Girl," who stays connected to the strong inner core of her individuality, comprised of her thoughts, feelings and desires. The Real Girl is not only able to listen to who she is, but to act on it. She learns to maintain a critical balance: she can manage the needs of others without sacrificing the integrity of her own.[8]

Many girls feel emotionally abandoned by their fathers. Although, in general, fathers have played more of a parenting role with their children in recent years, tight, busy schedules have kept many from developing close relationships with their children. Often, fathers' indifference to their daughters tells girls that they are unlovable and deserve to be abandoned or rejected. As girls repeatedly fail to command their father's full attention, their self-confidence can waver. Germaine Greer indicates that disappointments such as these can have life-long consequences, as young women's attitudes toward their fathers can easily generalize to other forms of authority. They may be attracted to abusive or abandoning men in their work or love relationships. Or, they may be unable to compete successfully in either work or social settings due to lack of confidence or persistent feelings of low self-esteem.[9]

My experience accurately mirrors Greer's description. The fear I developed in relationship to my father eventually generalized to other forms of authority. Prior to my involvement in twelve-step recovery programs, I was unable to speak up to or to assert myself with most of my supervisors, professors or older family members, regardless of whether they were male or female.

The Mother

The mother role is most familiar to women who grew up in the decades prior to 1970. Younger women who today choose to become either full-time mothers or caretakers will undoubtedly continue to identify strongly with the expectation for females to form relationships and give service. There are others, however, who, regardless of their age, have been conditioned and empowered to fulfill their ambitions and individual dreams, whether in a chosen career or avocation. For these women, the caretaking role discussed here may not have the same degree of resonance that it has had for me and the women of my generation. Whether or not it has been followed as a strict behavioral guideline, however, the mother/ caretaking role in our society has been primarily associated with women, and the behavior of all women has been influenced in a myriad of ways by its message. By examining this role, each woman can decide for herself its importance, as well as the degree to which it has impacted her in her daily life.

In an anecdote about the women in her family, specifically those of her grandmother's generation, Elizabeth Gilbert states:

> They cut up the finest and proudest parts of themselves and gave it all away. They re-patterned what was theirs and shaped it for others. They went without. They were the last ones to eat at supper and they were the first ones to get up every morning, warming the cold kitchen for another day spent caring for everyone else. This was the only thing that they knew how to do. This was their guiding verb and their defining principle in life: *They gave.*[10]

In this passage, Gilbert speaks to us about the legacy of selfless giving that we all share as women. My maternal grandmother lived her life as a homemaker and mother. When she was in her early seventy's, she would often say to me, "Dear, I am living today only for you grandchildren." My grandmother never stopped to think about how her statement reflected her inability to love herself. She died in the early 1970's, a decade before codependency was even defined as a concept.

There are numerous stories in the codependency literature that tell about women who are excessively sensitive to the needs of others. This pattern is often found among daughters from alcoholic or otherwise dysfunctional families. The stories tell of women who often are trying desperately to hold families together and to keep things going under stressful and almost impossible conditions.[11] Quoting Nancy Chodorow, Janice Haaken points out that in the alcoholic or dysfunctional home, the women's enabling is intrinsically connected to the moral dilemmas she confronts in her position as family caretaker. Women are more likely to be asked to justify their failure to respond to the needs of others, as opposed to men, who are more likely to construct arguments which justify their need to maintain social distance.[12]

Maryanne Walters describes codependents fitting the stereotypical description of women—over-involved, depending upon others for approval, not taking care of themselves, having poor boundaries, intoxicated with relationships, too willing to assume blame, putting the needs of others before themselves. Walters points out that, although 85 percent of the readers of books and pamphlets about codependency are women, these books basically describe the ways that women bring about their own self- destruction, even if they omit any discussion of the ways this self-destruction might be sanctioned by our society. Walters suggests that, while clearly intended to empower, the codependency movement and the self-help literature unwittingly present as pathological behaviors and personal characteristics that are feminine.[13]

Being sensitive to and providing for the needs of others, even at the expense of her own needs, is the emotional core of a woman's feminine role. Therefore, women who act on their own behalf, rather than for that of others, risk being seen as unfeminine. These qualities can be admirable when the "other" is someone, who, like a child, is younger or more vulnerable, but it becomes less understandable when the "other" is someone with greater resources. Middle-class femininity requires that a woman place the emotional needs of a male before her own, whether he is a fellow student, a colleague, a boss, a boyfriend, or a husband.[14] Yet, while women have taken care of men as nurturers, caretakers or helpmates, men have, in their theories of psychological development or economic systems, tended to devalue that care. When the masculine concept of individual achievement and maturity is equated with personal autonomy, concern

Elizabeth Ralston

with relationships is perceived as a weakness, rather than as a human strength.[15]

One of the organizing principles for women has traditionally been the sense that their lives should be guided by the constant need to attune themselves to the wishes, desires and needs of others. "Others" are, therefore, the important persons to consider, and their needs will be the guides for women's actions. This prescription leads to enormous problems, for it is supposed to be carried out as if women did not have needs of their own, as if one could serve others without simultaneously attending to one's own interests and desires. Carried to its logical extension, it produces the syndrome of the martyr and/or the smothering wife and mother.[16]

Because of this cultural edict, instead of being allowed to develop as far as they possibly can, women traditionally have been encouraged to concentrate on forming and maintaining a relationship to one person. As part of this process, they have been diverted from exploring or expressing their needs, but, instead have been encouraged to "transfer" their needs. This has often meant that they've come to see their needs as if they were identical to those of others—usually men or children. Traditional women who have managed this transformation and who have fulfilled the perceived needs of others, have been led to believe that they will be fulfilled.[17]

With the expectations of womanhood in America resulting in confusing double binds, it's not surprising that adult women have struggled with the same issues that overwhelmed them as adolescents. According to Pipher, "They come to lose weight, to save their marriages or to rescue their children. When I ask them about their own needs, they are confused by the question." Pipher adds, "Women often know how everyone in their family thinks and feels except themselves. They are great at balancing the needs of their co-workers, husbands, children and friends, but they forget to put themselves into the equation. They struggle with adolescent questions still unresolved: How important are looks and popularity? How do I care for myself and not be selfish? How can I be honest and still be loved? How can I achieve and not threaten others? How can I be sexual and not a sex object? How can I be responsible, but not responsible for everyone?"[18]

Carol Gilligan describes the problems that many women have in making independent decisions. She quotes a divorced middle-aged woman, mother of adolescent daughters: "As a woman, I felt I never understood that I was a person, that I could make decisions and I had a right to make decisions. I always felt that that belonged to my father or my husband in some way, or church, which was always represented by a male clergyman. There were the three men in my life: father, husband and clergyman, and they had much more to say about what I should or shouldn't do. They were really authority figures which I accepted.[19] Gilligan points out that the essence of moral decision is the exercise of choice and the willingness to accept responsibility for that choice. To the extent that women perceive themselves as having no choice, they correspondingly excuse themselves from the responsibility that decision-making entails.[20]

There is a remarkable correspondence between the characteristics of women playing out the traditional female role and the codependent "pleaser." Some of the characteristics of the pleaser are: 1) you have medium to low self-esteem; 2) you come from a family where your emotional needs were not met, particularly by your father; 3) you are attempting to create as an adult what was missing emotionally for you as a child; 4) as a child you attempted to be "daddy's little girl," you received attention for playing this role as a child and are still playing it today; 5) you feel that you can you can fix, reform and change him; 6) deep down you don't feel that you deserve to be loved or respected; 7) you are quick to blame yourself when something goes wrong; and 8) you may be part of the caring or helping professions such as social work, nursing or teaching.[21]

I recall several years ago speaking with a woman, a married mother of two, who I'd met at a twelve-step recovery meeting. She shared with me that she felt that what she did was not important, because she was just a stay-at-home mom. I responded by saying how very important I felt that her job as a mother was. Many agree that raising children is the most important job in the world. It's certainly difficult to imagine what our society would be like without the dedication of mothers. Yet, this vital contribution is, for the most part, considered unimportant and even banal in our society. Most take female care giving almost completely for granted. Like the woman I spoke with at the twelve-step recovery meeting, the assumption is that the job of making a home for a child and developing his or her capabilities is equated with "doing nothing."[22]

Yet, a group of new studies reveals that the amount of work involved in unpaid child care is far greater than economists ever imagined. It rivals in size the largest industries of the visible economy. By some estimates, even in the most industrialized countries the total hours spent on unpaid household work—much of is associated with raising children—amount to at least half of the hours of paid work in the market. Up to 80 percent of this unpaid labor is contributed by women. This huge gift of un-reimbursed time and labor explains, in a nutshell, why adult women are so much poorer than men—even though they work longer hours than men in almost every country in the world.[23] In spite of this, government social policies don't define unpaid care of family dependents as work. A family's primary caregiver is not considered a full productive citizen, eligible in her own right for the major social insurance programs. The only source of income for those caregivers who lose their source of support is welfare, and that is only if they have young children. For these and other reasons, motherhood is the single biggest risk factor for poverty in old age.[24] Elizabeth Warren, former law professor and current U. S. Senator, adds that women who are more likely to care for child dependents are three times as likely to file for bankruptcy as single women without children.[25]

Women and Power

From Supreme Court Justice to astronaut, over the past five decades, women have shattered significant barriers. Today, women who are able to reach their potentials and focus on their goals can achieve a great deal. Many even feel that gender discrimination has become a non-issue. So why, then should the issue of personal, economic or political power be a problem for women? Why should we debate these issues if, as some believe, we can really "have it all"?

In a 2007 magazine article, Arianna Huffington argued that many women continue to have an uneasy relationship to power as well as with the traits necessary for leadership. She described the dilemma of women who fear that if they are really powerful, they will be considered ruthless, pushy or strident—all epithets that strike at the core of our femininity.

Women are still working at trying to overcome the fear that power and womanliness are mutually exclusive.[26]

It is because of the ambivalence that women have with the issue of power that much of the research completed decades ago regarding this issue still seems relevant today. In a 1976 study, it was found that women who used direct forms of power risked gaining a reputation for being pushy, overbearing, unfeminine and/or castrating. Sources cited in the study indicated that women may have used indirect forms of power because they were explicitly trained to do so.[27] Paula Johnson, the author of this article, hypothesized reasons for learned helplessness in women. Historically, because women have not had the access to the amount of concrete resources that men have had, they've perceived themselves as less competent than men, underestimating their successes, knowledge, intelligence and logic. They've therefore often relied on helplessness in problem-solving situations, which, in a circular pattern, has led to lower self-esteem, especially in the ability to perceive themselves as persons of influence.[28]

Research conducted more recently demonstrates that our society's values regarding women and power have changed very little since the 1970's. In a 2007 study conducted by Victoria Brescoll, a post-doctoral scholar at Yale University, women who were judged to be angry were attributed the lowest status of those in four groups: men judged to be angry, men judged to be sad, women judged to be sad and women judged to be angry. A group composed of males and females gave the highest status to the men who were judged to be angry. In the experiment, the angry man was also assigned a much larger salary than those in the other groups. Conversely, the study participants gave angry women the lowest salary of the four groups. In a second, similar experiment, women who were unemotional were assigned a significantly larger salary by the study participants than angry or emotional ones, except in cases where there was shown to be a good reason for their anger. In contrast, regardless of whether he was angry or unemotional, the male executive was awarded the highest salary. The implication of this research shows that in order to be seen as rational, as well as viewed in a positive way by others, professional women do not often have the luxury to express their angry feelings openly.[29]

In a well-known thirty-year old study regarding sex differences and learned helplessness, a review of the literature indicated that boys confronted with a new task had expectancies of success that were higher than those that their past performance would warrant. Girls, on the other hand, tended to do precisely the opposite. Their expectations fell significantly below those of boys, even when their experience has been equally as successful as, or more successful than, that of their male counterparts. Another study showed that despite demonstrated competence, girls maintained unrealistically low opinions of their abilities. These opinions could influence their achievement-related behavior when they entered into new learning situations.[30]

Gloria Steinem illustrates some of the difficulties girls have developing self esteem after exposure to our educational system. She described research in educational settings, where boys tend to be praised for achievement, while girls are praised for interacting well with others. In other research boys were called on more often by classroom teachers and talked to more in their average response by a ratio of three to one. Despite this, the teachers, even ones who considered themselves to be feminists, perceived the girls as talking more. According to Steinem, this fact is indicative of the cultural bias that makes us feel that females talk too much, and that women should be "good listeners." In this research, the teachers were measuring the female students against those expectations, not reality.[31] In a cross-cultural study of classrooms in the United States and Great Britain, researchers found that boys are twice as likely to be seen as model students and praised by teachers, five times more likely to receive a teacher's attention, and eight to twelve times more likely to speak up in class than are girls.[32]

Despite the results of research such as this, women have made many in-roads, especially in the area of education. In contrast to most of the women in my generation, many young women today are in the process of seriously pursuing careers. Approximately 58% of college undergraduates nation-wide are female and the girl-boy ratio will probably tip past 60-40 in a few years. For African Americans females outnumber males by a margin of 2 to 1. Nevertheless, especially in some private colleges mediocre boys continue to be admitted over high-performing girls. While accomplished females were placed on the waiting list, less accomplished males would be accepted over them. When the fact of these unequal admissions practices were brought to the attention of young women, by and large, they tended to accept that this was the way that admissions processes work. One dean of admissions asked, "Why aren't they marching in the streets? It isn't fair, and young women should be saying something about it not being fair."[33]

It is unfortunate that women's relative successes in our colleges and universities have not been reflected as well in the workplace. Because many more women enter professional fields at the bottom, there is a naïve belief that they have been rising surely and steadily to the top. In a soon-to-be released report from the White House Project's Corporate Council, it was found that, although women comprise 50% of the population, they occupy only 20 percent of top-level positions in organizations. This percentage is much lower in the military and in Fortune 500 companies and higher in nonprofit organizations, where the salaries are low. This percentage is stable in the areas of politics, business, and journalism. Furthermore, in the area of political representation for women, the U.S. is 69th in the world, behind seemingly more conservative countries such as Iraq and North Korea.[34]

Despite the fact that women are now 50 percent of the workforce, they still do not receive comparable pay for performing the same jobs as men. Although they earn high college GPA's in every subject, a recent study by the American Association of University Women found that even just one year after college graduation, women earn only 80% of what men do. Overall the gap widens over time. The study found that Louisiana has the biggest pay disparity, with women aged 25 and over earning 64 percent of their male counterparts, while West Virginia has the least disparity in pay, with women earning 89 percent of the salary that men earn. Most of the remaining states ranged from approximately 71 to 77 percent that women earn in comparison to salaries earned by men. Motherhood has long been the explanation for this persistent pay gap, yet a decade out of college, full time working women who haven't had children still make less than their male counterparts.[35]

A recent ruling by the U. S. Supreme Court, declared that any individual who suspects they might be paid less than their counterparts must file a complaint under the main federal antidiscrimination law, Title VII, before they've been employed for 180 days. Unfortunately, this information is normally not made available to employees in work settings, and employers are not legally compelled to reveal it. Employees who are able to get information on salary differences most often must resort to getting it informally, from sympathetic colleagues at work. In 2009, to counteract these hidden abuses by corporations and small business owners, the Lilly Ledbetter Law was presented to both houses of Congress to make equal pay for equal work the law of the land. Named after the woman who brought her case to the U.S. Supreme Court after discovering that she had been a victim of gender-based wage discrimination during a twenty-three year career at Good-Year Corporation, the legislation was signed into law on January 29, 2009 by President Barak Obama.

Contrary to popular belief, women do not earn less money because they work less or are less interested in succeeding. In a longitudinal study of over 800 MBA graduates over a 16 year period, work values for men and women remained the same except that the women scored higher in the area of wanting to do an excellent job. There were no significant differences in wanting to help people or in power-related work values. Nevertheless, gender was a significant predictor of salaries, as the men earned more than the women. The researchers found that the differences in salaries were not connected to differences in work values between the women and men. The researchers found that gender explained almost 20% of the difference in salary levels.[36]

Most women in the labor force today work primarily because of the family's material needs. Divorced, single and widowed mothers must work to avoid poverty. Most women would not leave paid employment, however, even if the family did not need the money. Surveys of working class mothers indicate that these women are quite committed to their jobs. This finding may be explained in part by the social psychology of the workplace, its social support, adult companionship, and the contact with the larger world. This fact may explain why 56 percent of full-time homemakers say that they would choose to have a career if they had to do it all over again.[37] Another reason that women prefer to keep their jobs is that with rising divorce rates, they don't feel secure in giving up their full time employment, even if their pay is less than a man's. This reality is equally true whether they are mothers, or non-mothers. Women who fear for their marriages find the old means of economic support an insecure reality.[38]

A federally funded three-year study of 745 married women showed working women to be in better emotional health than those who are not employed. The research furthermore showed that women who increase their participation in the work force report lower levels of psychological distress, whereas those who lessen their commitment to work suffer higher psychological distress. A 1990 survey of depression in 1,000 families found that among the most depressed women were those who did not work and who stayed at home with children.[39] Thus, research has shown that paid work is good for women; work offers women a chance to increase their self-esteem, is a hedge against depression, and helps to create an improvement in over-all health and well-being.

Women do not have more heart attacks, nor is there any decrease in their life spans because of entering the work force. In fact, the National Center for Health Statistics reported in 1993 that a study of 13,000 women showed working women

Elizabeth Ralston

at lower risk of heart disease than non-employed women; the working women had lower blood pressure, lower cholesterol levels, and weighed less.[40]

Most women work one shift at the office or factory and a "second shift" at home. In an averaged time estimate of major studies completed in the 1960's and 1970's, Arlie Hochschild found that women in these studies worked roughly fifteen hours longer each week than men. Over a year, they worked an extra month of twenty-four hour days. Over a dozen years, it was an extra year of twenty-four-hour days.[41]

In recent years, however, men have begun to assume more of the domestic and especially the childrearing responsibilities in the home, thus, providing more relief for their wives. Even with supportive husbands who will relieve them of some of the burden, however, women tend to feel more responsible for home and children. More women reported feeling torn between one sense of urgency and another, between tending to a fearful child, or the need to show her boss she was "serious" at work. More women than men questioned how good they were as parents.[42] Data also show that when fathers share childcare responsibilities, thereby lessening this strain, the positive effects of employment on mothers' mental health is enhanced.[43]

Psychologists agree that married men report higher rates of satisfaction with their lives because they have had more areas of support for their well-being—home and family—than have women at home. By contrast, homemakers, who have often had the most boring, repetitive work, had no pay and no quitting time, reported much lower rates of satisfaction with their lives than married men. Women—even those who have been high-powered career women—can turn into doormats when they go home, running to do errands for husbands, children, in-laws and parents. Exacerbating the situation, when life at home isn't all that it was expected, women have blamed themselves. Women can avoid excessive guilt if they can look at the role of the housewife the way they would look at any other job, weighing the costs and the benefits of it. One of the ways to deal with feelings of little or no control or personal boundaries is to be able to say, "No." They can also realize when they need a break from the endless, repetitive housework and childcare and make sure that they get enough relief to avoid feeling stressed out. Occasionally paying babysitters or housecleaners with childcare and household tasks can be one important way to maintain mental and physical health.[44]

Finally, research has found that women who felt they had some control over their lives had a more sympathetic, less controlling mothering style than women who felt that they had little or no control. The results of the research imply that looking after one's own interests and intellectual pursuits may make one a better mother. In addition, it has been found that behavior which involves action and independence seems to be an essential ingredient for good emotional health. Therefore, getting involved in activities that increase the complexities of their lives and giving them the opportunity for this independent, action-oriented behavior would be important for the mental health of women at home. In summary, although it's long been our cultural ideal, the selfless, all-sacrificing wife and mother is a sure prescription for disaster.[45]

Some Final Thoughts

A danger for some women in recovery for codependency is that, instead of relating their long-standing relationship conflicts in relationship to an external cause, such as their financial, political or social circumstances, they tend to re-frame these conflicts, as residing primarily within themselves.[46] The opposite may also occur, where women may perceive their problems being caused solely by external factors. If they are unable to relate to a twelve-step program which emphasizes at least some internal causation, women may stop coming to meetings altogether. Cynthia was one of these women. I met Cynthia at a Co-Dependents Anonymous meeting. Although she had quit college in order to get married and start a family, she shared that her husband had divorced her after twenty years of marriage. Because she hadn't completed her degree and had no work experience, Cynthia took an entry-level job as an airline hostess after her divorce was final. Barely subsisting on her low salary, she was forced to live in a cramped, one room apartment. Living comfortably on his executive's six-figure income, however, her ex-husband was able to remarry and start a new family. After that first visit Cynthia never returned to our meeting. In my opinion women like Cynthia stop coming to meetings, because they can see no way out of living their lives ruled by a culturally enforced codependency.

We've all been exposed to these cultural expectations. Yet, when confronting gender-based codependency, women are often at a distinct disadvantage. Not only are women involved in intimate relationships with their husbands or partners, they're involved in multiple relationships with other males and females in family and friendship circles. Presumed responsibilities in these relationships may serve to reinforce traditional roles. Subtle pressure can arise from other sources, such as church, friendships or informal group settings. It is in settings such as these that women feel forced to accept certain "understandings" or "assumptions" regarding their responsibilities. We've all given into these pressures. When volunteers are requested to help out with a church potluck, or to organize an informal group party, it's not only the women who agree to step forward, it's most likely women who are *expected* to step forward. If a birthday or holiday is to be remembered, it's invariably a woman who runs to the store for the card or the present. If a child or an older relative need to be cared for, it's most often a woman who provides this service. If a child or a pet leaves a mess, it's likely to be a woman who cleans it up. By extending her caretaking role into the numerous areas of her life, it's possible that a woman could find herself mired in an existence almost totally dominated by the expectations of caring for others. It is these external factors, combined with an individual woman's reaction to them that can create entrenched codependent attitudes and behaviors. It is these "unspoken" and unacknowledged rules and "hidden" expectations that codependent women need to acknowledge and confront in order for them to feel more in control of their own lives.

Although much progress has been made in the area of equal opportunity for women, over the past decade or so, the perception spread by the media, as well as other sources, is that that all of the problems of gender bias have miraculously been solved. I believe this is far from the truth. We have a long way to go in the area of true gender equality. It is for these reasons that those of us that are seeking healthy rather than an unhealthy manners of giving, may need to periodically stop and weigh our actions. As we are likely to continue being asked to give from a variety of sources, women in recovery from codependency need to learn to differentiate the ways of giving that nourish them from the ways that make them feel burdened. As their right to the fulfillment of their healthy needs may be called into question, many women may have to stop and ask themselves seemingly simple questions, such as what they want or don't want, or, what they like or don't like. Then, they need to follow through on their understanding and demand the opportunity to have their needs met. Ideally, the goal of a woman's recovery should be to enable her to stand her ground, speak up and communicate to others who she is and what she wants on her own terms. It is though this process that women learn to understand who they are in authentic relationship with others.

Whether or not they are involved in a program of recovery from codependency, women need to learn to feel comfortable exercising their own power. Although socialized to feel uncomfortable dominating or exercising power over others, when they are are introduced to the concept of the power to accomplish for others, or for the good of the whole, women are much more willing to embrace their own potential for leadership. Author Gloria Feldt labels this type of leadership power-*to*, rather than the leadership we associate mostly with male leadership, or power *over*.[47] A 2007 study of women in the workplace published by McKinsey and Company management consultants entitled, "Women Matter," indicated that woman managers are more likely than men to make collaborative decisions, to behave as role models and to consider the ethical consequences of their acts.[48] Rather than forcing compliance through fiat or manipulation, this type of cooperative, supportive leadership focuses on providing solutions to problems; taking cues from this caring, transparent model, women hopefully will learn to feel more comfortable assuming leadership roles.

Despite persistent challenges such as concerted resistance and backlash, progress for women begun by the feminist revolution of the 1970's continues unabated. Whether or not they perceive themselves as feminists or just coming into their own, women need to understand that, to the degree that they are able to live up to their true potentials as adults and economic beings in our society, they are taking part in and are the direct beneficiaries of the progress begun by the feminists of the 1960's and 1970's. It's sometimes hard to remember that only sixty years ago there were no women reporting the news on radio or on television. There were no female orchestra conductors, movie producers or directors. Few women were doctors, lawyers, judges, mayors, governors, elected state or locally elected officials, U. S. congresswomen, senators or cabinet members. There were no women police officers, fire fighters, CEOs, soldiers, pilots, ensigns, astronauts, ministers or rabbis; there were only a handful of women academic professors, scientists, business owners, visual artists, authors or print journalists. Yet, over the past half century women have made unparalleled strides in all of these careers. They've become increasingly visible in politics and government, corporations, the arts and the professions.

In my opinion, all of these changes are nothing short of miraculous. And whether they would care to admit it, not one of the women demonstrating these changes could have shown the faith, self-discipline and self-sacrifice necessary to have achieved their goals by allowing themselves to be influenced by anything other than *de-facto* feminist goals.

Elizabeth Ralston

Over the last fifty years women have shown a remarkable combination of strength, courage, flexibility and resilience in handling the hugely complex social, economic and political changes that have impacted their lives. They are doing so now and will continue to do so into the future. Women have consistently displayed competence in a myriad of areas that is ever expanding, even as they continue to demonstrate the ability to care for and nurture others.

Yet, because of their cultural conditioning, when it comes to their own challenges, some women can face them with a combination of fear, ambivalence, anxiety or dread. When these feelings arise, it's important to locate their source. Even a superficial examination of her gender conditioning could provide a woman with some understanding of these contradictions and could signal the beginning of the healing process. Every woman, whether she is a caretaker, mother, student or professional woman, could benefit from this type of examination. By separating out the healthy from the unhealthy aspects of her gender role, a woman can learn to take responsibility, not only for the state of her being, but for her own happiness. In addition, she could learn to discern healthy and growth-enhancing from unhealthy pursuits.

Whether in improving in their assertiveness skills, in enhancing their communication skills, in participating more often in activities which bring them joy or in simply being able to acknowledge their feelings, women can find this evaluative process to be empowering and richly rewarding. Given the nature of their conditioning, they deserve no less.

Chapter 6

Men and Codependency

*As a boy I was taught from an early age that
"men don't cry" and, if they had feelings at all,
they certainly didn't show them. "Never allow
anyone to see your weakness because people will
ridicule you and take advantage of you."
"If you feel weak or hurt, you must hide that to
maintain your masculine image."*

From "Bob's Story"
In Co-dependents Anonymous

Boyhood

Prior to puberty boys appear to be just immature human beings, not unlike the girls in their classes at school. As boys develop, however, they are expected to become increasingly tough, hard-edged and emotionally detached. How this happens is somewhat of a mystery to me. And, although I understand that it does occur, I often find myself asking, "Are these unemotional, competitive and sometimes controlling individuals who men really are?" After reviewing vivid memories of my sweet, vulnerable nephews while they were growing up, I found myself answering, "No, not really."

Most men are kind and decent individuals. It is ironical, therefore, that masculinity is so often portrayed in a negative light. Through the pervasive influence of television programs and movies, we learn that a man must exercise power, aggression, domination, control and even ruthlessness in order to be masculine. This fact may explain in part why men regarded as the most masculine are athletes, police officers, members of the military, business tycoons and even gangsters.[1] All too often these hyper-masculine role models teach boys to control, conquer and manipulate, be physically strong, arrogant and detached from their feelings.[2] Television commercials alone often teach boys that a man is only a man when he is tough, drives a truck and drinks lots of beer.[3]

At some point in the mind of the growing boy, the biological reality of his "maleness" becomes synonymous with his sense of masculinity. Even for those who are intellectually aware of the difference between the biological fact of maleness and masculinity, the masculine ideal can be so overwhelming that it can be difficult for them to distinguish the individuals they might want to become (e.g., less sexist, more fully human) from the men they actually are. The tension between masculinity and maleness is intense because the concept of masculinity requires suppression of a whole range of human needs, feelings, goals and forms of expression.[4]

Whether or not it is intentional, emotional awareness tends to be discouraged in boys. Research indicates that mothers encourage talk about angry feelings more with boys and speak about sadness and distress more with girls. Other research shows that fathers are more rigid than mothers about guiding their sons towards traditional masculine patterns of behavior.[5] The boy code is learned everywhere: in sandboxes, playgrounds, schoolrooms, camps, churches and hangouts. Boys learn to keep a stiff upper lip, not show their feelings, act cool, tough, not be too nice, and, if someone punches you, you just laugh and brush it off.[6] These requirements can exhaust boys' energies, because it calls on them to pretend to be confident and tough even though they often feel afraid or unsure of themselves.[7] During this transitional period, weak, sad or dependent boys can be transformed into men who are rugged and independent who prefer to work, succeed and suffer alone, even while they share a portion of their lives with women.[8]

Adolescence

Especially in recent years, boys have received confusing and conflicting messages about the parameters of appropriate masculine behavior from society, their peers and even their parents. On the one hand, they are told that they should be cool, confident and strong. On the other hand they're told that they should be egalitarian with others (particularly with girls), sensitive and open with their feelings.[9] As a reflection of society's ambivalence about masculinity, these two opposing images of manhood can create confusion and uncertainty in boys regarding their appropriate masculine role.[10]

As they mature, boys can experience domination, humiliation, fear and betrayal; these are all by-products of "the culture of cruelty," a term first used by authors Dan Kindlon and Michael Thompson.[11] Despite appearances of shared loyalty and friendship, boys learn to live in fear in this "culture." They adhere to the "culture's" code, however, because by doing so, they believe that they will eventually be able to "measure up" to their internalized masculine ideal. Exposure to this "culture" produces boys who develop emotional guardedness, mistrust and wariness, instead of the empathy and trust necessary in developing healthy relationships. This emotional style can unfortunately characterize the manner in which many men approach relationships for the rest of their lives. Under constant pressure to assert power or else be labeled as a weakling, boys are more likely to show cruelty to others with little recognition of, or regard for, its emotional impact. Boys are cruel, in part because they are afraid of the judgment of other boys who may be quick to judge them as something less than masculine; their need to defend against that fear is ironclad.[12]

Boys report that they would like to maintain close and trusting relationships with their peers, even if they have previously experienced disappointment in friendships. Feminist researcher Niobe Way interviewed a group of 15 and 16 year-old boys in a longitudinal study regarding their friendships with boys their own age. Results suggested that as these boys grew older they grew increasingly distrustful of their male peers. By their latter-year interviews, the boys spoke about not having close male friends because they didn't trust their male peers. Many of them, however, yearned for close male friendships and recalled having had such relationships at earlier ages.[13]

As he grows older a boy is encouraged to detach from his mother as a major source of love and support. Although culturally enforced, this separation from his mother can be experienced as a terrible loss for a boy that may be even more difficult because his sisters are encouraged to remain in connection with her. The boy is rarely encouraged to acknowledge this loss through the grieving process; consequently, he may continue to long for a connection with his mother which he can never recapture.[14] Generalized to adult relationships, although young men can unconsciously yearn for closeness with women, because of their adherence to the masculine code, they will deny their dependence on them.[15]

Developmentally boys lag behind girls in the area of verbal expression. This fact, combined with the cultural edict against sharing feelings, tends to channel boys' emotional energy into action. When boys are excited and happy, for instance, they often get loud and physical; they shout, they jump, they run, they push and shove one another around and run it off. When the emotions are too painful, however, a good run isn't good enough. Unable to "talk out" the emotional pressure, boys typically act out through verbal or physical aggression that walls them off emotionally from others, straining or severing emotional connections to the people and circumstances they find painful.[16] Other researchers have reached other conclusions, believing that the pattern of behavior often observed in adolescent boys of what psychologists call the "boy brain"—kinetic, disorganized, maddening and sometimes brilliant behaviors may be, at least in part, hardwired.[17]

Boys are frequently more emotional than they will report. In a poll of 1,000 teen-agers conducted for *Ms* Magazine in 1997, although 28 percent of young women aged fifteen to twenty-one stated that they felt depressed daily or several times a week, 20 percent of young men in the same age group reported feeling depressed with the same level of frequency. In addition, it's probable that boys may have been under-reporting the actual incidences of depression because of their reluctance to confess to feelings of sadness or vulnerability. Some of these boys may not only have failed to report, but may not even know when they've experienced depression.[18]

Elizabeth Ralston

Other studies have found similar contradictions. In a recent study of the secret love life of teen-age boys, a team of female social scientists found that at least some of the stereotypes attributed to boys are true: They scare easily, they're reluctant to talk about their emotions and then they do talk, they're awkward at it. However, in a sample of 1,316 boys and girls from the seventh, ninth and eleventh grades, the researchers found that boys were at least as emotionally invested in their romantic relationships as their female partners. In in-depth interviews, the boys' responses were passionate and forthright. The picture that developed from the data was very different from society's perceptions about the reality of the emotionally unresponsive male. This is not the type of information that boys would share with other boys. One boy confided to the researcher that he would never talk to his friends the way he talked to her, because his friends didn't have the feelings that he has.[19]

Transition to Adulthood

According to sociologist Michael Kimmel, the passage from adolescence to adulthood has evolved from a brief period to a separate stage of life which can potentially last two full decades, beginning at puberty and ending at around age 30.[20] Caused by a variety of factors, young men are beginning a family and taking on the responsibilities associated with a career later in life. Since the 1950's the average age of marriage has been increased by over four years for men, to age 27.4 and over five years for women to age 25.8.[21] Related to this problem, annual earnings for men ages 25 to 34 with full time jobs declined 17 percent from 1971 to 2002. This pattern has been exacerbated by globalization, which has caused an erosion of high paying manufacturing jobs, with an accompanying increase in low paying service-sector jobs.[22] These changes have understandably created confusion in the minds of many young men as to exactly what a man is and how they can become one.

Kimmel describes young men who appear directionless and clueless who rely on their peers to usher them into adulthood and validate their masculinity led by a set of rules known as "The Guy Code," (a close relative to the "boy code" mentioned earlier) a set of attitudes, values and traits that tells young men what it is to be a man. Its primary theme restricts men to never show emotions or to admit weakness. The face the young man shows to the world insists that everything is fine and under control. To keep his behavior in line with the code's standards, the young man's peers act as a kind of "gender police," constantly checking up on his behavior, making sure that he never strays into the imaginary line of feminine behavior.[23]

Throughout this process the young man who is heterosexual comes to define his masculinity primarily as a negative, as in *not being feminine,* or associated with women. In effect, from a young man's perspective, masculinity is fairly strictly defined as the *opposite* of femininity. From a psychodynamic perspective, a young man learns to reject and deny any deep personal involvement he may have had with his mother by repressing his feminine characteristics and by belittling those feminine characteristics he meets in the outside world.[24] Hyper-masculinity in males has been interpreted as a sign of insecurity. Extreme masculine behavior can thus be viewed as a defense against an insecure male identity, and as a way men can reject in themselves an identification with their mothers.[25]

During this period a young man's world view is dominated by his sense of masculine entitlement. This attitude is characterized in large part by a code of silence, a code which ensures that young men learn to support and conform unconditionally to the "Guy Code" by not confronting one another for excesses, bullying and/or violent behaviors. Reinforcing complicity partially through a system of shared shame, the code of silence extends a sense of protection to perpetrators, where behaviors such as excessive drinking and physical and/or sexual assault may go unpunished and appear to be condoned by other young men, as well as adults in positions of authority. Silence from those involved or aware of abuses is normally interpreted as tacit approval.[26] One of the most important hallmarks of the "Guy Code" is the concept of sexual conquest. Especially on college campuses, many young men engage in sexual predation and date rape because they perceive themselves to be entitled to power over women and women's bodies. By doing so they gain approval from other guys who view the domination of women as an important masculine rite of passage.[27]

Men's abuse of other men is also an integral part of patriarchal culture, from high school locker rooms to college fraternity hazing to military basic training. The man who takes abuse without complaint improves his chance of being accepted as a real man who deserves to share in male privilege. The man who objects risks being ostracized as a sissy, a mama's boy who can't take it.[28] In fraternity initiations young men often subject themselves to abusive, degrading and often dangerous behavior in order to "prove" themselves worthy of membership in their desired group. Although infrequent, deaths have occurred during these hazing incidences. Several years ago, for instance, a young man died from alcohol poisoning because he was forced to consume excessive amounts of alcohol during a fraternity initiation. Death by hazing is not a recent phenomenon. In the 1930's, my maternal uncle, only 22 years old at the time, died ultimately from injuries sustained from being clubbed on the stomach during a fraternity hazing at a well-known university in Philadelphia.

The Manager

The heroic male character so often seen on television and in the movies serves an important cultural purpose. Physically flawless, muscular and quick to act, he seems to have a timeless, mythical quality, serving as a model for men who may perceive themselves as down-trodden, especially during periods of cultural and/or economic upheaval. Heroic male characters are independent, self-assured and immensely focused characters who prevail in spite of enormous obstacles and challenges; they are unafraid of taking action. The masculine hero reinforces the principle of masculine privilege and dominance. In order to maintain their heroic status, however, these figures can normally associate with women only superficially and usually only during brief romantic interludes.

An alternate version of the heroic male model is that of the soldier/warrior. Often, men give of themselves in times of war, enduring severe hardships under dangerous circumstances without complaint. Some return home maimed or psychologically damaged; others pay the ultimate sacrifice of loss of life. In order to acknowledge the sacrifices of these brave men, as a society we have collectively understood that they should be honored and, if they die in combat, memorialized.

Elizabeth Ralston

With the "soldier/warrior" a bond has been created between manhood and warfare which affords a special status to the warrior; in the minds of many the soldier role is considered to be the ultimate proof of manhood. This understanding has become embedded in our national consciousness and is affirmed and accepted by most without reflection. A warrior's privileged status comes with a price, however: the unambiguous knowledge that in order for a "real" man to maintain his status as a warrior he must not only separate himself from women, but reject most "feminine" characteristics in himself.

I've often been confounded by the notion that those who can easily accept the idea of giving the ultimate sacrifice for home and country in time of war can have a difficult time extending themselves emotionally, arguably, a much easier task. As I collected information for this chapter, I was struck by the idea of all young men, regardless of their backgrounds, being trained to be "good soldiers." I perceived a tradition of warfare where generations of men have been conditioned as potential "warriors," to either fight and/or die as actual soldiers, or to take part in competitive "battles" for survival in the marketplace. Whether the source is from a military/warrior or heroic male model, men are trained to become masters of domination, action, competition and control. Whereas soldiers may possess genuine body armor, the traditional male, who has not served in a time of war, may not have physical body armor, but has effective mental and emotional armor, nonetheless; whether military or non-military, the male must manage, be in control and dominate. Playing either the "warrior" or "hero" role can severely restrict the degree of trust and caring that one man can assume in relationship to another and can be psychologically draining. It's possible that the self-destructive patterns of men who've played this role over long periods of time might have developed, at least in part, from their inability to relax from the seemingly endless struggle of competitive "battles" with other men.

The purpose of this chapter is to examine the development and the degree of influence of the hyper-masculine male role, otherwise known as the traditional male role, in our society. The traditional male role possesses numerous positive traits, such as discipline, strength, independence, assertiveness, courage and the willingness to assume responsibility. In order for a man to maintain this role in its present form, however, he must maintain a polarization between himself and women, as well as an emotional distance from other men, which can serve to stunt healthy social and emotional development. Although many men may relate to the hyper-masculine role with difficulty, its examination is nevertheless essential, given the deep and pervasive influence it exerts on all men in our society, particularly in the areas of gender conditioning and gender relations.

Operating under a predictable set of idealized rules for men set by the parental culture, the traditional male restricts his range of freely expressed thinking, feeling and behaving. This type of restriction is the central theme of earlier definitions of codependency and reflects the rigid, oppressive pattern of thinking that characterizes the codependent male.[29] A man guided by the rules of idealized traditional masculinity locks himself out of his emotional center, learns to either dominate or be dominated; there can be no in-between. The extremely macho male learns to deny the real importance of self through the blind obedience to the dictates of a hyper-masculine ideal.[30]

Although the traditional male role is not as clearly codependent as the female version, it has obvious codependent features. They are, among others, the need to be in control of others, the need to repress feelings and the need to seek validation from other men regarding a man's masculinity. In general, a traditional male tends to be a dominant codependent and avoids seeking help for his problems in living in either traditional psychotherapy or twelve-step recovery programs. Traditional males tend to view problems as residing outside of themselves and often resort to blaming others for their difficulties.

Men tend to ignore or overlook the problem of codependency in themselves because it forces them to look at behaviors that are bound up with their sense of manhood. Viewed another way, many of the typical "masculine" characteristics that make men feel they are men are also codependent behaviors. A group of counselors were asked to list codependent behaviors that they frequently saw in men. The list included the following behaviors:

1. Acting in an over-controlling manner; he must always do things *his* way.
2. Behaving like a workaholic.
3. Rescuing, protecting.
4. Lacks emotional expression.
5. Exhibits a fear of intimacy.
6. Often has a problem with addiction.
7. Lacks spirituality.
8. Uses other males for ego-strength.
9. Is externally validated only by what he does.
10. Exhibits extreme rigidity.
11. Overly asserts his masculinity.

Men who over-identify with the traditional masculine role tend to be codependent because, although they know the ways and preferences of other men, they cannot find appropriate answers for themselves.[31] Life for such men is often narrowly defined, constricted by extreme limits of permissible thinking, feeling and behaving. The extremism of the traditional macho (hyper-masculine) male meets the codependency definitions for rigidity, oppression and lack of emotional honesty.[32]

Because a man's concept of himself as a man must be "proven" in competition with other men, it's almost impossible for him to really truly know whether he's "made it" as a man. Often men try to prove their toughness and masculinity through feats of physical stamina, sexual prowess (by treating women as sex objects), and through the ability to handle various forms of intense pain. This pervasive sense of uncertainty undoubtedly has contributed to excessive bullying, hazing and other destructive types of behavior found among young men on school campuses, all in the name of an almost unattainable and elusive masculine ideal.[33]

According to Allan Johnson, the need for men to separate from women serves two primary purposes: it helps men to feel solidarity with other men, and it also enables them to assume a superior position in relation to women. Although this process enables men to form a stable masculine sense of self, the rejection of feminine characteristics ensures that men maintain connection with women in a conflicted way. As men learn to reject feminine qualities, not only do their inner and outer lives become more limited, but the process alienates them from their feelings and their bodies; in addition, this process deprives them of powerful inner resources designed to help them to cope with stress, fear

Elizabeth Ralston

and loss. Because patriarchy defines masculine identity by success at *not* being like women, men cannot honor and develop those aspects of themselves they most associate with women, as well as with their childhood connection to women. That so many men feel confused, incomplete, and resentful is inevitable under these conditions. Often, men hope that women can somehow make everything better.[34]

Psychologist Herb Goldberg has compared the process of encouraging many men to feel their feelings with that of asking a crippled man to run. The defenses that a man develops against expressing his feelings produces such massive defenses *against* them that he lives in constant reaction against himself. Typically, when he describes his feelings, he is in denial: "I'm not angry," "I don't feel like crying," "I don't any need help," are commonplace phrases. What he appears to be on the outside is superficial, a defense against what is really is on the inside.[35]

A hyper-masculine man is uncomfortable with the idea of going into therapy because it involves an admission that he might need help. As his perceived locus of control resides inside of himself, he cannot admit to feeling out of control, helpless or inadequate in any way. As a consequence, many of these men will wait until an emotional crisis has occurred before they can admit that they need help. Going into therapy is a way for a man to acknowledge that not only does he *not have* to handle all of his problems on his own, he *cannot* handle all of his problems on his own.[36] Many men, such as those in twelve-step recovery programs, have discovered that they can't function fully as men by ignoring their rage, frustration, vulnerabilities, or sorrows. Whether or not they care to admit this fact, men have a sensitive and emotional part of themselves that needs to be cultivated in order for them to lead more complete and healthy lives.[37]

Ron is frustrated over a situation at work. Ron's wife, Ann, notices that he is quieter than usual and seems depressed. When she asks him if something is wrong, he responds, "Nothing, I'm good, I'm good. Things are fine." In reality, Ron has always had problems owning up to feelings that may make him appear vulnerable, or "less than" other men he knows. When he lets his feelings build up, however, he can become irritable at home, easily finding fault and sometimes yelling at Ann for no apparent reason. Rather than admitting his feelings of vulnerability, he either represses his feelings, or displaces them on to Ann. After a month or so of this behavior, Ron is finally able to open up to her about his feelings of anxiety regarding his problems at work.

Like Ron, although the ordinary man is able to loosen up on the "controls" somewhat and reveal parts of his private self, because of his masculine conditioning, he does not do this very easily. The rules of the game for most males don't allow these situations to be acknowledged very often. The average man is only able to switch from the public, outer image to the private, inner self awkwardly and with the fear of vulnerability. Because these feelings can make a man feel inadequate, he may view them as a threat to his sense of masculinity. Although the roles the average male can play are more flexible than those of the extremely macho male, the difference in the ability to be open and vulnerable between the two is only one of degree.[38]

In father-son relationships, fathers are more successful who gently help their sons with the hard tasks of growing up rather than try to harden or toughen the boys to match a tough world. Boys who are the most prone to break down when the going gets tough are those who have been raised with the idea that to admit vulnerability, even to themselves, is to be weak.[39] In a study of family relationships, Researchers found that fathers generally related to their sons in three ways: as a leader or teacher, as a promoter or booster, or as a disciplinarian. Fathers were reluctant to give up leadership and control to adolescents regardless of their gender. When challenged by sons, however, many fathers would react with anger and a desire to regain control. In general fathers didn't react to daughters with the same level of antagonism as they did to their sons. With each passing year, a father's attitude typically becomes more protective of his daughter and more competitive towards his son. Given these findings, it's not surprising that teen-age boys often have a difficult time talking to their fathers about emotional issues.[40]

The problem of men's relationships to their fathers was touched upon in the ground-breaking mythopoetic men's movement, led by poet Robert Bly, which began in the 1990's. The movement encouraged men to deal with feelings of loss and grief in relationship to emotionally distant or physically absent fathers. From Bly's perspective, this unresolved grieving process could leave a man with a negative, wounded image of his father, an image often transmitted to him by his mother, who herself may have prejudiced feelings towards the father.[41] In this movement's gatherings and retreats, men were able to talk about their strong feelings for their absent fathers in the presence of other men. The meetings encouraged feelings of male bonding and community and encouraged an openness to sharing feelings with other men. This type of experience was often difficult for men to regain in other areas of their lives.[42] As part of the healing process, each man was encouraged to get in touch with his inner "Wild

Man," named after the main character Iron John in Bly's book by the same title. Iron John is an archetypal figure of manhood representing wildness, the irrational, intuition, emotion, the body and nature.[43]

In a critique of Bly's mythopoetic philosophy, sociologist Allan Johnson has contradicted Bly's criticism of mothers, whom he has viewed as constricting their sons' healthy development by being possessive and overly protective. Johnson argues that traditionally, it was fathers and not mothers who were given the authority to civilize children, as mothers were considered to possess a weaker inner moral character.[44] Johnson also notes that Bly shifted the blame away from a patriarchal system towards single mothers, who, being abandoned by distant fathers, are merely reacting to the void created by their absence.[45]

Men often expect a degree of toughness from themselves that they do not expect from women. During a rainstorm not long ago I hesitated with two male friends until we finally ran outside to the car. While my one friend carefully shielded me with his umbrella as we walked together to the car, he called out to the other man to "make a run for it." When I confronted both of them on the double standard between my treatment and my friend's in getting to the car, the first man turned to me, and laughed, "You don't understand. This is a guy thing." The second man, who had run through the rain without an umbrella, nodded in complete agreement. Although an innocuous example, this masculine attitude of needing to be "tough" is typical for many men.

Whereas the basic processes, attitudes, and behavior patterns that are life-sustaining and health nurturing are commonly identified as feminine, at their most extreme traditional masculine values can be viewed as self-destructive,

Elizabeth Ralston

especially when it comes to the care of a man's physical health. Many hyper-masculine men who are ill are embarrassed to acknowledge it and will deny their illness as long as possible.[46] Goldberg explores this theme in showing how men often avoid normal healthy responses because these responses are associated with femininity. As a consequence, many cannot perceive their own levels of stress, self-poisoning, fatigue and emotional pain. Their early conditioning as men has numbed that awareness and has made it anxiety provoking to give in to them, even when they do experience it.[47] A hyper-masculine man does not allow himself to give in to any kind of obvious self-nurturance. At his most extreme, the hyper-masculine male may reject activities such as sleeping, relaxing, expressing emotions, asking for help, paying too much attention to diet, especially when not sick, abstinence from alcohol, self care, dependence on others for help, touching in non-sexual ways, as excessively feminine.[48]

Because he has difficulty expressing his feelings, the hyper-masculine man may exhibit behaviors that are unpredictable, negative or risky, such as wild driving, binge drinking, violent outbursts and destructive affairs. . . He may experience emotional disturbances such as depression, withdrawal, anxiety and pseudo-euphoria, which can mask unexpressed, repressed feelings. He can be subjected to many psycho-physiological disorders such as backaches, headaches, fatigue and ulcers. He can numb himself with alcohol or drugs. His defenses against his feelings force him further and further from relationships; as a consequence, he becomes increasingly lonely and alienated, with a deepening sense of futility about them.[49]

Many men spend time in "male identified." environments. In local bars, sporting events and workplaces men are the most vulnerable to the judgments, spoken or implied, of other men. When a man suspects himself of being less than a real man, he judges himself from the perceived attitudes of other men. When he is accused of being a "wimp" or of otherwise failing to measure up, this idea almost always comes from another man that he knows. This understanding contradicts the widely held belief that the key to a heterosexual man's sense of manhood is held by a woman.[50] A patriarchal society creates an environment which makes men fear what other men might do to them, how control might be turned on to them to do them harm and deprive them of is most important to them. Men are afraid of all of the things that other men can do to exert control and thereby protect and enhance their standing as real men in relation to other men.[51]

Traditional men learn to take part in aggressive male banter, always have the answer and never admit to being wrong. While they do this, they will keep their feelings to themselves. Often men will go out of their way to avoid the appearance that women can control them. They pump iron, go hunting, play football, or engage in martial arts. Although they may deal with their fear and inspire it in others, they still maintain an underlying commitment to men, what men do and the system that binds them together. Since patriarchy is organized around male-identified control, many men protect themselves from the fear of losing control, by increasing their own sense of it. Participation in this cycle of fear tends to lock men in an endless pursuit of and defense against control, for under patriarchy, control is paradoxically, both the source of and the solution to men's fear. . . It's a curious irony that the more in control a man tries to be, the less secure he feels.[52]

Men who are achievers often develop a dominant parental pattern with their partners. He needs to be in control so that he can dominate the relationship, but at the same time he is usually dependent on his (usually) female partner to nurture the emotional side of the relationship. Although he needs this nurturance, he often has difficulty giving it back. The achiever often intellectualizes, looks good and does all the right things. He may be excessively detached but not "in" the relationship. Frequently he may feel that something is missing in the relationship; instead of searching inside of himself, however, he often looks outside of the relationship to discover the source of the problem. Although the achiever can possess many positive characteristics such as competence, reliability, success in career attainment and self-motivation, he can possess other, more negative characteristics, such as being a perfectionist or being overly competitive, inexpressive, tense and rigid and lax in self-care.[53]

As mentioned earlier, a traditional man does not normally come into therapy until he has reached an insurmountable crisis and has exhausted all other remedies. This creates a resistance to taking part in the therapeutic process.[54] What he wants most, to be understood and accepted for who is really is, is often sabotaged by his need to protect himself from the unknowns of his inner self. Typically, he is so disconnected from his inner self that he doesn't really trust it.[55] Both influences—the larger parental culture and the traumatic reactions of having lived in a dysfunctional family—teach men to cover up and to protect themselves. The long-term result is that it is normal for many men to never really develop a fluid sense of themselves as emotional beings.[56]

Over the past three decades because of a combination of losses in employment and stagnant wages, as well as the more recent losses in employment due to the 2009 economic down-turn, middle-class men have experienced an erosion of their role as primary breadwinner, as potentially difficult as those challenges suffered by women in relationship to their quest for equal rights. But, unlike women, who've felt empowered to express their concerns, in the case of men, the reticence has been overwhelming. Why the silence? Where is the outrage? Why is the reaction of the middle-class man been so muted with regards to his potential economic disenfranchisement? In truth, it appears that by not complaining, men have conformed flawlessly to their conditioned role; to not complain, to express their anger and fears, or, amazingly, even to mention their feelings about their diminished status in one of the primary roles that has traditionally defined them as men. Perhaps if they were to admit that they do not have everything "under control," they would lose their "masculine" status in the eyes of other men. And so, they remain silent, fearing to experience the feelings related to losses in relationship to their traditional role.

Regardless of his need to play the dominant "manager" role, the average man has played the non-dominant "subordinate" role many times throughout his life. In addition to playing the subordinate role in relationship to a "dominant" father, another sphere of activity where most men have experienced subordination is at work. Since the American management system has been based on a ranked, power-over model, it has often fostered an adversarial relationship between management and employees. Employees are often taught that they have few intrinsic rights and are valued only as much as their skills match those needed by the corporation at any given time. In most work settings employees who disagree with employers are not encouraged to be explicitly confrontational. Most employees learn that their opinions are rarely valued; among the rank-and-file workers, independent thinking and creative problem-solving is rarely encouraged. Those groomed for management are often asked to work excessively long hours and to focus on their jobs to the detriment of their family lives. A similar pattern can be found within academia, where the assistant professors at universities are often asked to take on full teaching loads and help undergraduates with academic counseling, as well as manage to publish in professional journals.

Except for those at the very top echelons, all men have experienced the enforced subordinate codependent roles which are encouraged and fostered by impersonal and at times dehumanizing work environments. After a lifetime of experiencing these subordinate experiences, most men are well acquainted with playing the non-dominant codependent role.

Although some men may have difficulty relating to various aspects of the hyper-masculine male role, all men have had extensive exposure to this traditional male role, and most likely exhibit some characteristics of this model even if they are unaware of it. From such innocent behaviors such as "forgetting" to take one's medications, making medical appointments or resisting asking for directions, to more blatant ones such as excessive drinking, sexist attitudes towards women, or seeking to dominate others' behaviors, most men can relate to at least some aspects of this role. The pressure on them to fulfill its injunctions may feel overwhelming. As they work on their gender role issues, many will discover that their relationships with women, as well as those with other men, will improve. Some will experience fewer needs to dominate others. Many will come to accept that they're only human; through working on their gender issues they will come to understand that, although they can feel fallible, helpless, dependent or insecure, they can still remain men.

Revisiting Manhood

Men would do well to examine the cultural messages that have conditioned them to take part in unhealthy and outmoded attitudes and behaviors regarding their sense of manhood. They may have spent years as addicts or alcoholics, or they may have dominated their wives, girlfriends and/ or children, which may have caused ruptures in these relationships, or they may have had crises in their mental and/or physical health. Some men may never begin these self-examinations because they may experience doubts connected to their manhood early in the process. Nevertheless, these critical junctures could force many to radically examine the hyper-masculine ethic, as well as all of the ways it has negatively impacted their lives and the lives of the women, children and other men that they know. Although this work may be daunting and disorienting, it could force men to radically change the way they've been taught to perceive themselves in relationship to their world; these turning points in their lives might force them to radically examine the hyper-masculine ethic, and all of the ways it has impacted not only their lives, but the lives of the women and other men that they've known. Even if a man conducts his self-examination in isolation, he should know that he's not alone in attempting this process.

As Dan Mulhern, law professor at the University of California at Berkeley and husband to the former governor of Michigan, Jennifer Granholm, stated in a letter to his son, "Men today do not have clear social roles to inherit, and often . . . have to talk, negotiate, sacrifice and make it up as they go along," Mulhern adds that, "A modern warrior prevails not by sheer physical strength, but by exercising his values with discipline." He states further that in relationships with the other sex a man honors a woman best when he treats her as an equal, ". . neither unduly backing down, nor asking her to give up her principals and experience."[57]

It's critical to also acknowledge the millions of men, quiet unsung heroes of our culture, who go about their lives with an attitude of responsible cooperation with others regularly and on a daily basis. These men vastly out-number those who approach life's challenges in a conflicted way, needing to exert power over others in order to achieve their goals. Because these men may seem more "normal" than their conflict-laden neighbors, their behaviors may seem unremarkable and can be easily overlooked. Our news media's tendency to stress negative events throughout the daily news cycle may make it appear as though these men are in the minority, rather than representing the majority of men. For many of these men examining the traditional male role and how it impacts their lives may not present a major challenge.

Regardless of their backgrounds, however, a critical examination of their masculine role could lead men to experience fewer conflicts with regards to their gender role, rather than more. A review of their conditioning could enable men to maintain its healthy and positive aspects, while allowing them to eliminate the unhealthy elements, which may have had a negative impact on themselves and others. This process could result in an increase in self-acceptance and a growing tolerance for a wider range of behaviors that they could consider appropriately "masculine."

As difficult as making these changes can be, men can begin by making them in stages, starting with the most obvious behaviors, first. Whether his initial goal is to diminish his need to control others, to relate to women in non-sexist ways, or to learn to acknowledge hidden emotions such as anger, grief or fear, a careful examination of his gender conditioning could help a man accelerate his growth in the recovery process, as well as to develop healthier relationships with his family, friends and others in his community. To the degree that a man can develop the humility necessary to accept both his true limitations as well as his true potentials, examining his conditioning as a man can be a liberating process that could enable him to experience his shared humanity with women and other men in a deeper, more comprehensive way than he's ever imagined.

Chapter 7

The Hand and the Glove

No, no; only lean on me; I will advise you and direct you. I should not be a man if this womanly helplessness did not just give you a double attractiveness in my eyes.

Torvald

I have existed merely to perform tricks for you, Torvald. but you would have it so. You and papa have committed a great sin against me. It is your fault that I have made nothing of my life.

Nora
From *A Doll's House*
By Henrik Ibsen

At Opposite Ends

A dominant/non-dominant pattern may be appropriate and would be dependent on the particular situation. Whereas, a parent correctly setting limits for a three year old child is an appropriate dominant/non-dominant pattern, that same parent setting the same limits for a 35 year-old son or daughter may be inappropriate. Although a manager may manage during the working day, this same style might be inappropriate if used in a relationship with his significant other at night. While giving or taking orders would be appropriate in a military setting, this ranked style of behavior may not be appropriate for a less formal set of relationships. The key to assessment is whether the ranked behavior is appropriate to the situation and whether or not the individuals can extricate themselves from the pattern in a healthy manner once it has served its purpose for both of the individuals involved. This chapter will examine ranked relationships that are more or less permanent, and not those based on a temporary status which is capable of change, such as an employment role or developmental roles which are based on age and level of maturity and/or education.

Although my examination of polarized relationships has been mostly from the perspective of relationships between women and men, it's important to remember that the dominant/subordinate polarized relationship can exist between any two individuals, regardless of whether the relationship is based on gender, or some other set of factors. Regardless of their gender, all individuals play a submissive role while growing up, simply because children begin their relationships as subordinates. Our society is rife with these polarized relationships. Familiar examples include dominant parents and subordinate children, dominant older siblings and subordinate younger siblings, dominant employers and subordinate employees or dominant teachers and their subordinate students. Although we think of ourselves as members of an egalitarian society, these polarizing relationships are probably far more common than any of us would care to admit. In my opinion codependent behaviors are found especially on either end of the dominant/non-dominant spectrum and are found within the framework of polarized relationships. These ranked behaviors are often the result of years of conditioning, and tend to be exhibited by individuals automatically, without conscious planning.

In fixed ranked relationships between any two dominant and subordinate groups, members of the dominant group will tend to label members of the subordinate group as defective or substandard in a number of ways.[1] Subordinates are often defined as less equal by characteristics ascribed at birth. In addition, the actions and words of the dominant group tend to be negative towards the subordinates. Dominant groups define the parameters of acceptable roles for the subordinates, which usually involve providing services that no member of the dominant group wants to perform for him or herself. Functions that a dominant group prefers to perform, on the other hand, are carefully guarded and closed to subordinates. Subordinates are usually said to be unable to perform the preferred roles, as their incapacities are unchangeable, and further development is impossible. This myth of incompetence can be challenged by circumstances outside the relationship, such as the necessities of World War II, where women, presumed to be incompetent, skillfully assumed the jobs of absent men in the war factories.[2]

Subordinates are encouraged to develop personal psychological characteristics that are pleasing to the dominant group. These characteristics form a cluster of similar behaviors such as submissiveness, passivity, docility, dependency, lack of initiative, an inability to act, to decide, to think and to act from a position of maturity, strength and competence.[3] In the process of controlling those of the subordinate group, dominants have to justify control and protect themselves from an awareness of how this control affects those in the subordinate group. Therefore, controllers come to see themselves as subjects who intend and decide what will happen, and to see those less dominant as objects to be acted upon. It's not surprising, therefore, that subordinates have little opportunity to develop qualities outside of their prescribed roles. Characteristics such as intelligence, initiative or assertiveness on the part of subordinates will either be ignored or will be considered anomalous by dominants.

The dominant group has the greatest influence in determining a culture's outlook, philosophy, morality, social mores and even its science. Thus, as part of society's guiding concepts, the unequal relationship becomes legitimate.[4] Prohibited from acting openly and directly to get what they want, members of the subordinate group will resort to disguised and indirect ways of acting and reacting. Subordinates tend to avoid direct, honest reactions to negative treatment, as well as proactive, open action based on self-interest. One significant result of this indirect behavior is that members of the dominant group are denied the ability to receive important feedback about how their behavior affects others. Dominant group members are also deprived of valuable information about subordinates. Although subordinates will rarely directly confront the dominants, to survive, they know much more about them than vice versa. They become highly attuned to the dominants to the point of being able to predict their reactions of pleasure and displeasure.[5]

Men and Women

The average man may feel powerless in relationship to some women, as, in comparison to him, these women may have socio-economic and educational advantages. It is partly for reasons such as these that many men resist seeing themselves as part of a privileged group. We forget, however, that in contrast to a woman, a man who is devalued because of his social, ethnic or economic status is not devalued because of his *maleness*. For women, however, gender oppression is linked to a cultural devaluating of femaleness itself. Women are defined as culturally inferior because they are *women*.[6] Many times girls and women will express their subordinate status with gestures and words; they may avert their eyes or lower their voices while speaking, particularly with males or anyone in a position of authority. Showing empathy and support in relationships, they tend to be "nicer" than their male counterparts. By rarely speaking harshly to or challenging others, women's "niceness" often serves to maintain the status quo.[7] My experience while growing up certainly copied this description. Timid as a girl, I was afraid of becoming involved in arguments or otherwise calling attention to myself. Although I was unfailingly pleasant and "nice" to almost everyone I knew, I felt powerless and ineffectual with those in authority, especially if those authority figures were men. I almost never expressed anger and was afraid to even admit to having angry feelings. For some women being "nice" can become so habitual that they are unable to communicate disagreement or anger even when it's clearly appropriate. When issues arise that are worth fighting for, women often become paralyzed, unable to tolerate the disapproval that their opinion might generate.[8]

Under these circumstances, a woman may not be able to use her power and strength to operate independently and to take responsibility for her own life and experiences. Her dependent attitude can lead her to feel that she has no personhood. At the same time she may blame the man in her life for depriving her of her sense of identity. Even when supported or encouraged by him, she may continue to act passively and unassertively, is often unable to clearly define herself or her preferences, and, when confronting problems, she will tend to react rather than act. Such women may suffer from psychosomatic complaints or chronic fatigue; these symptoms stem from repressed feelings of resentment from being overly controlled.[9] Women who are discouraged from expressing anger or aggression directly may perceive themselves as helpless victims. Their unexpressed anger often presents itself in indirect ways such as forgetfulness, procrastination, misunderstanding, lateness, nagging, withholding affection, depression, moodiness, listlessness, compulsive mothering and homemaking, sexual manipulation, blaming, inciting guilt, acting helpless and self-righteousness.[10]

In the introduction of a 1976 study mentioned in Chapter 5, Paula Johnson found that women were expected to use indirect forms of power, and that women who used direct forms of power risked becoming labeled as pushy, overbearing, unfeminine, and/or castrating.[11] Over thirty-five years after this study was published, expectations for females in the area of assertiveness have changed very little. For example, Presidential candidate Hillary Clinton was consistently given a low likeability rating during the 2008 Democratic Presidential primary campaign in comparison with her opponent, Barak Obama. Many of her supporters felt that this was because she spoke in a direct, forceful and assertive manner which was not characteristic of our cultural image of "appropriate" female behavior. Where females are concerned we still haven't decided how much power we can tolerate. In school environments, for instance, we ask girls to walk a fine line between being both strong and likeable. This is a line we typically do not concern ourselves about with boys.[12]

One way for a man to maintain his hyper-masculine or "macho" image is to view first girls, and later women as sexual objects to be manipulated. Another of his beliefs is that women like being told what to do by men in order to "keep them in line."[13] In order to maintain the belief that he is strong, a hyper-masculine man must maintain an illusion that women are weak.[14] Although the core principle of control is part of what defines manhood, control does not define womanhood. Women, as subordinates, are not as encouraged to pursue control, and those that do will often be criticized.[15] It is ironical that it is by becoming submissive that a women bestows on the man his full status as a man. In this sense it is a woman's acquiescence to submission (to a subordinate status) which has the power to create a man's full strength.[16]

Rather than examine our true values regarding the nature of power, we often reinforce the culturally mandated belief that income, status and control over others are the most important hallmarks of power. Women are therefore more likely to marry men with that image. In doing so, they will most likely relate to these men as subordinates.[17] Conversely, some men fear that without the traditional masculine success symbols, they will become progressively unlovable and sexually unattractive to women. These men are therefore caught in a double bind, castigated for their power and success orientation and rejected when they don't have them.[18]

One of the most difficult aspects of the relationships between the traditional masculine and feminine roles is the dependency it fosters. The role of the dominant male cannot exist without the submissiveness of the non-dominant female, and vice versa. This circular form of dependency keeps the relationship in a codependent state where each controls the other through his or her behavior. If you can make your partner dependent on you in some way, then he or she can't stray too far away. Husbands, for instance, can make their wives dependent by controlling the family finances, while wives make their husbands dependent by taking care of their personal needs, such as laundry and cooking.[19] These roles, at opposite extremes, complement each other in unhealthy ways. By placing the male in the role of the actor who decides and controls, and the female in the role of the reactor who does not decide or control, the man and woman are doomed to be linked together neurotically; one cannot exist without the other. In order for the man to control, he must have a woman who is willing to be controlled. Women who are too assertive would be unacceptable for him, and men who are too passive, egalitarian, or open-ended about decision-making would be unacceptable for her. Dominant males tend to shy away from women who are too assertive, tending to be attracted to the more passive "feminine" women. Nevertheless, such men may eventually come to feel resentful because they find themselves taking part in one-sided interactions, where they feel compelled to always dominate and control.[20] Conversely, a submissive female is often attracted to a dominant male because he can help to guide her in areas where she may be weak, such as in proactive decision-making.

Examining a couple's pattern of negative interactions requires self-reflection on the part of each partner. For example, if one player blames the other for doing something he or she despises, it may be productive if each member were to look within him or herself to discover what was being done to encourage that player's detested behavior. By paying excessive attention to the other's dysfunctional behaviors, the complaining player may be reinforcing and, by doing so, unwittingly helping to create those same behaviors.[21] This type of interaction is really a circular dance in which the behavior of one partner maintains and provokes the behavior of the other. The circular dance has no beginning and no end. In the final analysis, it matters little who started it. The question of greater significance is: "How do we break out of it?"[22]

The Role of Romance

With its emphasis on melting, merging and losing boundaries the romantic relationship is an ideal source of codependency. Being in love fosters codependent behaviors such as making decisions in deference to your future partner, spending excessive time pleasing and/or improving yourself for your potential or present partner and feeling that your basic problems would be solved if your loved one would solve his or her problems. Romance creates codependency by maintaining the myth that your sense of well-being is determined more by the state of your love life than by your *own* life. When romance blooms at a distance, bursts into obsession and then diminishes into ordinariness—or perhaps unrequited pain. . . it can become an addiction and is a cycle which can be repeated again and again.[23]

Romance helps to create and maintain polarized gender roles. When boys and girls are taught that certain parts of themselves are appropriate only to the "opposite sex," they will look for those lost parts of themselves in other people. Once adolescence arrives, this lack of a true self in both sexes, this feeling of being incomplete and perhaps also ashamed of parts of oneself that "belong" to the opposite sex, can create an urge to construct a false social persona; this tendency can be exacerbated by the intensified gender expectations of our society. In search of inner wholeness, young men and women will try to absorb and possess someone else.[24]

While in love, both the man and the woman believe that the relationship is all that exists, and that the relationship will somehow "save" them. This myth of romantic love teaches us that the man and the women should somehow be answerable for every aspect of each other's joy and happiness. If they choose to marry, the couple soon learn that their job description as spouses will be to become each other's "everything."[25]

In his book *The Road Less Traveled*, M. Scott Peck describes the phenomena of "falling in love" as a sudden collapse of the individual's ego boundaries which permits one to merge his or her identity with that of another. The dramatic decrease of loneliness accompanying this collapse is experienced by most of us as an ecstatic event. We and our beloved are perceived to be one. According to Peck, falling in love is not an act of will nor is it a conscious choice. He describes it as a phenomenon where we develop a feeling of omnipotence not have experienced by most of us since childhood. Since all things seem possible to us, we temporarily believe that the strength of our love will cause all of our problems to be overcome.[26] Peck hypothesizes that falling in love may be a genetically determined instinctual component of mating behavior, which serves to increase the possibility of sexual pairing and bonding, and by doing so, increase the probability of the survival of the species. Put another way, according to Peck, falling in love may be a trick that our genes pull on our minds in order to trap us into marriage.[27] The myth of romantic love from fairy tales tells us that there is only one man for a woman and only one woman for a man, and that this has been predetermined "in the stars;" this is a common theme which Peck believes to be completely false.[28]

According to Peck the qualities of true love have little in common with those of our romantic ideal. Although they include the ability to relate to another with caring, attention and empathy, these characteristics are also balanced with the ability to relate to another as an independent and separate being.[29]

Cultural messages from plays, musicals, movies, novels and television programs, reinforce the illusion of health and power of the romantic relationship. Descriptions of euphoric highs, extreme dependency and feelings that the relationship will last forever are endemic and predictable in all of these *genres*. Unexamined, these mythical codependent relationships are described as highly desired states, even though lovers can suffer terribly because of them. While listening to country-western music, for instance, it's not uncommon to hear singers lament that their lives are over now that their lovers have gone. Over and over again we are instructed by these cultural models that the depth of love can be measured by the pain that it causes, and that only those who can truly suffer for love, truly love. The overwhelming popularity of these types of messages may be due in part to the fact that there is more drama in an unhealthy relationship than in the more subtle but stable emotional qualities of a healthy one.[30]

Finally, the romantic ideal creates the illusion that an intrinsically unequal relationship between a man and a woman is, in fact, an equal one. Although the state of "being in love " presumes equality between the sexes, once married, the "traditional" relationship most often develops into a connection defined largely by rank. In the traditional "perfect marriage," the man is the one who deals with the outside world, makes the money, decides how the money will be spent and makes all of the important decisions. In doing so the man also sees himself as taking care of the "little woman."[31] Even if the woman makes many mundane decisions, the man must still have the final say on how these situations should be handled.

Economic Inequality

In our society gender roles are changing, but slowly. Men still expect to dominate in areas of job importance and salary increases. In a 2001 study, although it was estimated that 78% of workers are married to employed spouses, and in 75% of these cases, both spouses were employed full time, men who found increases in their own salaries to be rewarding, viewed increases in their wives' salaries over their own in a negative light. When men's salaries increased over time over their wives' salaries, the men's positive perception of their marital role increased with their increase in salaries.[32] Yet, from recent media reports we are led to believe that a woman can achieve anything that a man can economically. Although in recent years the media has painted a picture of economic parity between women and men, ten years after college a woman will earn only 69 percent of what a man earns.[33] In 2008 the median income for women was $36,000 a year, 23 percent less than that of their male counterparts.[34] Finally, unlike what we read and hear in the media, women are still segregated into low paying jobs; forty-three percent of women were confined to twenty occupational categories where the median income is just over $27,000 per year. Despite the fact that more girls than boys are now attending college, most women continue to be tracked into low-paying "pink collar" jobs that pay inadequately.[35]

The disparity in earning potential ensures the continuation of inequality in the male/female relationship. Where dual-earner couples are concerned, a cycle is set up that works economically in favor of men and against women. Because men put more of their male identity into work, in economic terms, their work time is worth more than commensurate female work time. A man's leisure time is more valuable than that of the average women, because of the greater relative value of his work time; his leisure therefore enables him to refuel his energy, strengthen his ambition and move ahead faster at work. Because he does less at home than a woman, he can work longer hours while at work, prove his loyalty to his company and get promoted faster. As a man's aspirations expand, so does his pay. The inverse is true for a woman. As the woman carries less of her identity in her job, her work comes second, and she carried more of the second shift, thus providing backstage support for her husband's work. Because she supports her husband's efforts at work more than he supports hers, her personal ambitions tend to contract, rather than expand. Already lower than his, her earning capacity rises more slowly. The extra month a year that she works contributes not only to her husband's success, but to the expanding wage gap between them, and thus serves to continue the cycle.[36]

Emotional and Verbal Abuse

Countless studies by psychological researchers have demonstrated a direct relationship between traditional femininity and masculinity and the presence of low self-esteem and self acceptance. Inflexibility, dogmatism, competitiveness, aggression, distance from any female quality or person, homophobia, even cruelty and violence, become the classic gender masks of low self esteem in men. Submissiveness, dependency, need for male approval, fear of conflict, self-blame, and the inability to express anger are classic gender masks of low self-esteem in women.[37] Jealousy can spring from these feelings of inadequacy and incompleteness, and can increase as self-esteem diminishes. The more incomplete we feel, the more obsessed we become with owning someone on whom we've projected all of our missing qualities. This cycle, which begins with gender roles and ends with feelings of low self-esteem, can be a dangerous one. In a 1990 study of abusive relationships, it was determined that it is precisely when men and women more rigidly conform to traditional roles that abuse is most likely to occur.[38] The presence of stereotyped gender roles can reinforce these behaviors in both men and women; not only do they force females into a submissive and subordinate status with males, but, according to a 1993 study, authoritarianism, in conjunction with sex role traditionalism, was positively and significantly correlated with sexual aggression in men.[39]

Like countless others of my generation, I was counseled by my mother that the success or failure of the marriage relationship depended mostly on the woman and her ability to "make things right." Although my former husband was aloof and emotionally distant, I assumed that I was at fault for his behavior and blamed myself for his callousness and lack of responsiveness. Our relationship was accurately mirrored in the book, *The Pleasers.* The "pleaser," the female non-dominant partner, often comes from a family where her father did not meet her emotional needs; consequently, she is attracted to a man who reminds her of her father. The pleaser's (often unconscious) need to be dominated dove-tails with her dominant partner's need to dominate. The pleaser's low self esteem allows the controller to keep her off balance emotionally and in her place. He is counting on her to maintain her low self-esteem, so that she will continue to feel "less than" in relationship to him. Idealistically, she often hopes she can either fix or reform him; she may feel that he will eventually change to meet her needs. When he doesn't change, she takes the blame. He is quick to lay the blame on her; she accepts it and continues to feel inferior. She asks for very little and is grateful for small favors; he gives as little as possible and is counting on the fact that she will continue to feel unworthy in relationship to him. He will lie, be demanding, verbally dismissive or abusive because she'll take it and expects it. Although she's always trying harder to please, he lets her know that her efforts are never good enough.[40]

Where verbal abuse is present, the victim's perceptions are often undermined or discounted by the abuser. Because she is blamed, negated and is turned into a scapegoat by the abuser, the victim learns to tolerate abuse and loses self-esteem without realizing it.[41] In her research on the effects of verbal abuse, author Patricia Evans found that the abuser and the victim often live in two totally different psychological realities. The abuser's orientation was toward control, dominance and power over, whereas the victim partner's orientation was toward mutuality and co-creation.[42] Because the abuser will often deny that his behavior is abusive, the victim can be made to feel that she is not really experiencing abuse, if the verbal interaction does not occur when others are present. Women can often be attracted to abusive partners because of role-modeling provided by their parents. Beverly Engel shares a family recollection of one of her clients, a victim of emotional abuse:

> My father was clearly the one in charge. My mother seemed to be defined by him. Her whole life was centered around what he wanted from her, and she waited on him hand and foot. If she pleased him she was rewarded by his affection, but if she angered him, he would withdraw and not speak to her.[43]

Never having experienced the self-acceptance and security of real personal power, the male abuser avoids his feelings of powerlessness. In order not to face his own feelings, he cannot admit to his need to dominate, manipulate and control.[44]

Regardless of the gender of the two individuals involved, relationships based on domination are inauthentic. They are characterized by inequality, manipulation, hostility, control and negation and not equality, partnership, good will, mutuality, intimacy and validation.[45]

Sexual and Physical Abuse

Crimes of sexual assault against women are endemic in our society. One woman in six in the U.S. has been a victim of sexual assault.[46] Other sources report a statistic closer to one in four. It's not easy to prove rape, and the victim is often blamed for helping to create the event either by her dress or actions, should she decide to press charges. Fortunately, a group of early feminist researchers were instrumental in redefining rape as a crime of hate and violence which enforces the subordination of women, rather than merely as a sexual act.[47]

Sexual trauma has reached epidemic proportions for women in the military —with numbers twice as high as in the civilian population. Consequently, women returning from active duty are reporting signs of mental health issues at a higher rate than their male counterparts. In most of these cases the perpetrators have been American male soldiers. Not only are these offenses inadequately investigated or punished, the response of the military authorities in response to female soldiers' complaints is telling: sit down and shut up. Where women are concerned, it's the hyper-masculine military culture that needs to change.[48]

Women are not the only victims of sexual assault in the military. Confidential reports filed in 2010 indicate that reported sexual assaults on men by other men in the military have increased three times since 2007. The Pentagon has belatedly begun to admit the problem of sexual violence against both genders, as men screening positive for "military sexual trauma" has increased from 30,000 in 2003 to nearly 50,000 in 2011. The high rate of assaults against women in the military has helped to shed light on assaults against men. The Pentagon admits that these reported incidents are only a small percentage of the number that actually occur. Military experts and outside researchers indicate that perpetrators are usually heterosexual, which underscores the awareness that sexual assault is not based on sexual attraction, but on an ethic of domination and violence.[49]

The military's hyper-masculine culture confers manhood on its members and romanticizes the soldier as a war hero. In the minds of many this fact makes him incapable of doing wrong. Because of this, victims, rather than perpetrators, are often blamed. In cases where women are raped or assaulted, many feel that the "hero" perpetrator must have been enticed into it by his victim. In cases where men have been raped or assaulted, many may assume that victims have been lying as a way to smear the perpetrator for their own selfish purposes.

Because commanders can exercise discretion when meting out punishment, many rapists are never penalized, even when the victims have followed all established procedures in reporting the offense.[50] Overall, only a small percentage of sexual assaults in the military are ever reported. Perhaps more victims of both sexes would come forward more often if they believed that they would be treated fairly by the military's judicial system.

Regardless of the gender of the victim, crimes of sexual assault are also under-reported outside of the military. Women are victims of sexual assault more often than are men, and. when offenses against women occur, they are often downplayed by the media and by those in positions of power. Because these are male on female crimes and often a consequence of domestic conflicts, the importance of them is often lost, even on the victims themselves. Many times, the victim is blamed for the offense, as in statements such as, "She must have asked for it," or "She must have had it coming." And yet, if crimes were reported having occurred between members of any two *other* groups in our society (such as between two different ethnic groups, or gay versus straight) they would not only be discussed in numerous public venues, but they would also be widely reported by the media as hate crimes. This tepid response on the part of our legal and political leaders, as well as under-reporting of these incidents by the media in a wealthy nation such as ours is, in my opinion, an unsupportable pattern to maintain against half of its population.

Regardless of the gender of the victim, downplaying or under-reporting sexual assault is psychologically dismissive and gives victims the message that they can't do much about these crimes when they do occur. Insulating the public from the full extent of these offenses gives the message that they are either non-existent or are merely a figment of the victims' imaginations.

Finally, individuals who report rape or sexual assault must demonstrate a considerable amount of courage. Attacking victims for speaking out on such matters only serves to highlight the callousness of the attackers. Under circumstances such as these, an individual should never have to apologize for the right to speak out, either in their own defense, or in the defense of those they care about.

Breaking the Circular Pattern

Denise took the role of co-chair for her twelve-step recovery group's annual retreat with Carl. About half-way through the retreat preparations, she recognized that she was doing an inordinate amount of behind-the-scenes work, such as shopping for food and supplies, paying the bills, ordering coffee mugs, organizing the fundraising auction and formatting and mailing flyers. Carl volunteered to do the more visible and "important" jobs such as picking out the speakers for the speaker meeting, introducing the speakers during the opening exercises and being the M.C. for the afternoon auction. By the end of the retreat, Denise felt drained and exhausted, whereas Carl had enjoyed himself immensely. After examining their respective roles, Denise came to understand that without recognizing it, she and Carl had divided their tasks along traditional gender lines: he was the one who appeared to be "in charge," while she had assumed the role of his overworked but under-appreciated "helper."

As the case of Denise and Carl, we can automatically fall back on the expectations of culturally endorsed gender roles that may operate beneath the radar of our full conscious awareness. Sometimes these expectations can be carried to absurd lengths. Male friends will routinely hold my door or my chair at a restaurant, gestures born of an age-old, but anachronistic tradition which held that delicate ladies should be protected from such "difficult" tasks. Although we all know better, these quaint traditions persist. When alone, or in the company of other women, I open my own door or push in my chair without a second thought. Women seem to live a sort of double life: weak when men are present, but strong and competent when they aren't. Conversely, men can become unaccountably helpless in a kitchen when women are around, unable to either lift a plate or set a table. Although some of these patterns may undoubtedly be unconscious on our parts, when they do seep into our conscious awareness, it's important to confront them as we are willing and able. Although bringing up the fact that I am capable of opening my own door at a restaurant may elicit an embarrassed laugh from my male companion, I can still search for a way to confront this issue in a manner that can begin a healthy dialogue between us regarding deeper issues involving gender.

Unconscious patterns can inhibit healthy relations between any two codependents, regardless of gender. Bob's older brother, Jim, is in charge of the family business, and Bob is "second in command." Jim is such a "manager," however, that Bob doesn't get a chance to learn his own

Elizabeth Ralston

management style, learn other important aspects of the business or to even confront Jim about these facts. "Things get done much better, when I do them," opines Jim. When Jim was laid up in the hospital after a car accident, however, Bob was not ready to take over. Unprepared by his brother, and unaccustomed to confronting him about this fact, Bob floundered. Bob's professional growth was hobbled by Jim's unconscious need to play the role of the domineering older brother, long after this role had outworn its usefulness.

Breaking out of our conditioned roles can be frustrating. As a woman I've been routinely advised that, in the event of an emergency, I need to be able to change a car tire by myself. I recall attempting this once, only to discover that the lug nuts on the tire on had been placed there with a pneumatic wrench. This mechanical device had made it impossible for me, as a woman, to loosen the nuts on the tire with an ordinary lug wrench. In this situation asking for help from a (usually male) mechanic to remove the lug nuts unfortunately only served to exacerbate my feelings of helplessness.

In other ways, non-dominants have found themselves compelled to radically change their behavior in order simply to survive. Because the verbal inhibitions I had learned as a girl were handicapping me professionally, I made a persistent effort to speak up in as many settings as I could. Although I felt afraid, I doggedly forced myself into work and volunteer situations where I had to speak to others. After twenty-five years of verbal "practice" I now find myself able to speak fairly easily in public. In order to save my professional life I had to challenge the status quo; many others in recovery have had to change in similar ways.

These changes do not come easily. At one point I was so overwhelmed by the sheer magnitude of them that the best that I could do was to focus on one behavior at a time. Each time I modified my behavior in a particular area, I took a risk: a risk of not being listened to, or, of engendering anger and of being punished in some way. For me, taking responsibility for making decisions was especially problematic. Since, as subordinate, I had normally been "advised" what to do, I had rarely experienced the emotional challenges connected with making a difficult decision. Because I had taken so little responsibility, if a decision went wrong, I rarely had to examine my part in it. At first, I found the process excruciating. Either I would be consumed with worry or I would procrastinate in taking action. Somewhat belatedly, I came to learn that, although I don't have to perfect at making decisions, I still have to make them. By giving myself permission in this open-ended way, I finally started to feel like an adult in the area of decision-making. I've started to take responsibility for my successes and have learned to do the same for my failures. My learning curve has been huge, but nonetheless humbling, and from my mistakes, I've learned pitfalls to avoid; nevertheless, in the area of decision-making, I still consider myself to be a work in progress.

Whether the polarized relationships are between a man and a woman, or are between any other two individuals, partners must alter their accustomed roles in order to stop the circular and codependent pattern. Since the capacity for mutual agreement on these matters is unlikely in an unequal relationship, usually one of the pair must voluntarily stop playing his or her accustomed role first. When change occurs, it is usually (but not always) initiated by the non-dominant partner, often after he or she has been involved in either individual or group therapy, or in a support group such as a twelve-step recovery program.

Transitioning non-dominants may also have to bear the burden and take the risks that go with being defined as "troublemakers" in making these changes. This process may be frightening for the non-dominant, who seeks to try healthier communication patterns, as well as the dominant, who may be threatened by changes in the status quo. Many have found confronting or expressing anger to be especially threatening, as this process can turn covert tension into open conflict. Although this type of risk-taking may be unsettling at first, the rewards can be tremendous. Years ago, I discovered that it was much easier to incur another's wrath by asking for what I needed, than by never asking and gaining nothing at all.

Changes by non-dominant women may produce fear in dominant men. Miller points out that efforts by women to challenge their traditional roles are often met with resistance by men, who misinterpret these efforts as attempts to diminish them and their masculinity, as well as their ability to feel in control. Miller adds, however, that such a skewed relationship is an inappropriate one for two adults to take part in.[51] Some men may also fear that women will not stop with the need for equality. Why wouldn't they demand dominance? Some men may reason that if men have never been content with the concept of equality, why should women?[52]

Yet, despite their sometimes-convoluted nature, relations between the sexes do seem to be changing. I've noticed significantly more numbers of young men walking babies with strollers and taking care of toddlers at the park not far from my home during the past five years than I have in previous years, particularly when I compare these numbers to those

I observed as early as ten years ago. Along with the reports of men who are opting to stay at home while their wives work, observations such as mine have added to a growing awareness that many men have become increasingly flexible regarding their definition of acceptable work.

According to research of three hundred working couples completed in the 1990's, men and women as two earner couples today were gradually becoming equal partners. The most striking example was in the changed mutual style of parenting. According to the study, mothers and fathers no longer played entirely different roles in their children's lives. Both were deeply involved in nurturing their children from infancy on. In addition, both men and women enjoyed the same things about being parents. The researchers found no gender differences between men and women in the area of childrearing.[53]

In virtually every area of our society men and women are attempting to re-negotiate the rigid parameters of ranked relationships, held in place by centuries of tradition. The "weak" woman paired with the "strong" man encourages the worst form of enabling and entrenched codependent behaviors. In order for such a neurotic relationship to continue, both parties must wear blinders: blinders that shield them from the true potentials of themselves as well as those of their partners. In the area of gender relations, it's important to learn to think outside the box. Both women and men could continue the progress by experimenting with and trying out new behaviors not considered typical for their respective genders.

As with many other connections in transition, where relations between the genders is concerned, the female "hand" no longer fits into the male "glove" as it once did. Conversely, many men have found that living the life of the traditional male can be like trying to wear an ill-fitting straight jacket. As our transforming culture has accelerated commensurate changes in our behavior patterns, these changes have evolved out of necessity and stem from the daily vicissitudes of our lives. It's questionable that each time a woman or a man challenges traditional gender stereotypes by achieving a new milestone, either in the private or public sphere, that this change should, by definition, represent either a threat to the masculinity of men, the femininity of women or to the core values of our society. Those who make these changes are not deliberately challenging men, women, or even our cultural concept of the natural order of things. Although largely unaware of this fact, they are challenging patriarchy, a social institution already in transition, and they are doing this by simply demanding to be who they really are and by attempting to live up to their true potentials.

Chapter 8

The Healthy Relationship

*I learn to see myself as equal to others. My new
and renewed relationships are all with equal
partners.*

Promise 6 from the Twelve Promises of Co-
Dependent's Anonymous

Self Love

It's often been said that you cannot love another person
until you learn to love yourself. Among individuals seeking
emotional health, most would agree that one should strive to
develop a healthy relationship with oneself before beginning
a relationship with another. It's unfortunate and ironic that in
our society that we are often encouraged to initiate close and
intimate relationships with others before we have established
an essential self-affirming relationship with ourselves.

Co-Dependents Anonymous clearly acknowledges the
importance of one's relationship to oneself In its Twelve
Promises. Promise Five states, "I know a new love and
acceptance of myself and others. I feel genuinely lovable,

loving and loved." Promise Nine states, "I acknowledge that I am a unique and precious creation." Finally, Promise Ten states, "I no longer need to rely solely on others to provide my sense of worth."[1] Although fairly straight-forward, these promises are often difficult for codependents to implement, when they have spent their entire lives focused on meeting the needs of others before their own. As codependents, we must learn to attend to our own needs as if we were caring for another. Put another way, we must learn to become our own guides, mentors and best friends. Rather than mere selfishness, partnership with yourself means to be sensitive to yourself as well as others.[2]

According to John Bradshaw, one method to enhance self-love is to learn to become more assertive. Unlike aggressiveness, assertiveness is not shame-based behavior. A pre-requisite of assertiveness is being able to identify what our rights are with the expectation that they will be fulfilled. Not only does assertiveness allow individuals to defend their rights as human beings by asking for what they need, throughout this process they learn to set limits by being able to say, "No." Bradshaw suggests that we each create an individualized Bill of Rights, and give ourselves total permission to have these rights. These might include rights such as the right to any feelings which you may experience, the right to change your mind, the right to not have to explain or justify your behavior to others, the right to make mistakes and the right to not seek the approval from others. These rights would be especially useful for individuals who play submissive codependent roles.[3] Throughout the process of becoming more assertive, codependents learn that they can handle life's challenges without approaching them in a fear-based manner. Although sometimes a normal reaction to stress, fear should never be the core impetus which drives an individual to take action on her or his behalf.

Same Sex Groups

Traditionally encouraged to focus their energies on their families, or to compete, rather than to cooperate with other women, many women have difficulty relating themselves as part of a larger group made up of women, who share similar problems and challenges in life. Whether or not they care to admit it, all women share a common history and common roots. By learning to accept themselves unconditionally, women can learn to accept other women, as well. Although from different backgrounds, women can begin by accepting what they have in common. Some women are developing a new spirit of appreciation for themselves and other women based on egalitarian principles. This spirit is very different from evaluation and judgment along narrow lines. A ranked system might evaluate other women based on external factors such as how well dressed they are, whether and to whom they are married or how many children they have. Subordinates in a hierarchal society are often encouraged to judge one another in ways similar to these.[4] Women who seek to increase their awareness in this area may wish to begin their individual recovery process by connecting with other women in group settings, such as twelve-step recovery groups, therapy or personal growth groups or informal groups formed as part of a religious or political organization.

As mentioned in Chapter 6, while growing up men learn to compete with one another in the all-male environment sometimes known as the "culture of cruelty." Although bonding among men is encouraged as a way of maintaining male centeredness and male identification in our society, many relationships among men are based on mistrust and, at times, ruthless competition, attributes used to create individual and corporate wealth. In same-sex groups men could learn supportive ways of relating to one another, based on mutual respect and trust. They could establish empathy and concern for other men through communicating their thoughts and feelings, rather than by simply taking part in shared activities, as is more typical for men. As with women, such a group for men could be a twelve-step recovery group, a therapy group, a religious, or political group, or a men's group formed for personal growth.

The Healthy Relationship

M. Scott Peck describes some of the characteristics of a healthy relationship by stating what love is not: love is not dependence on another; nor is it merely the feeling of love, or self-sacrifice. In stating what love is, Peck describes it as, among other things, a committed action towards the growth and well-being of another. One type of love through action is by giving attention to another by listening to him or her. Although listening is most appropriate in a committed relationship such as marriage, he adds that few couples ever truly learn to listen to each other.[5]

According to John Bradshaw, there are four states to the intimate relationship. The first stage of being in love, he described as the codependent stage. The second stage, of power struggle, is the counter-dependent stage. The third stage of self-actualization is the independent stage. The final stage of co-creation is the interdependent stage. In this last stage the couple is clearly together because they want to be and not because they have to be. Rather than clinging together to make a whole, each member is confident about the integrity of his or her own separateness. After the couple has separated in order to truly become individuals in stage three, they come back together in the fourth interdependent stage to share intimacy. By doing so, they have attained an expanded awareness, a creation of their interdependent love, and a synthesis of the two individuals' unique ways of being. While each partner remains unique, the intimacy which they achieve in this stage is more constant, workable, deeper and more soulful than the ecstasy experienced in the "romance" of stage one.[6]

In agreement with Bradshaw, Peck describes genuine love as a state that not only respects the individuality of the other, but actually seeks to cultivate it, even at the risk of separation and loss. From his perspective, it is not the merging, but the separateness of the partners that enriches a union. A primary characteristic of genuine love is that the distinction between oneself and the other is always maintained and preserved. The genuine lover always respects and even encourages this separateness and the unique individuality of his or her loved one.[7]

In a healthy relationship, personal power emerges ideally from an individual's connection to his or her own feelings and increases through cooperation with, and participation in life. Cooperation with another individual who is also grounded in his or her own feelings generates or brings into being a shared reality. Understanding their own personal power, both partners are mutually supportive and empathetic of one another.[8] Coming into the relationship as whole and separate individuals, both partners are secure in their relationship to themselves; therefore, one partner does not need to exert control over the other. The following are some characteristics of this healthy relationship: 1) to bring one's thoughts and to hear the other's, 2) to express one's enthusiasm and to delight in the other's, 3) to reveal one's self and to reflect the other, 4) to value one's self and to esteem the other, 5) to pursue one's growth and to nurture the other's, 6) to protect one's self and to comfort the other, 7) to be one's self and to let the other be, 8) to love oneself and to love the other, 9) to follow one's interests and to encourage the other's, 10) to involve one's self and to assist the other, 11) to cherish one's solitude and to honor the other's.[9]

Kahlil Gibran, in his book, *The Prophet*, has written the following about a healthy relationship between two partners:

Love one another, but make not a bond of love:
Let it rather be a moving sea between the shores
Of your souls.

Fill each other's cup but drink not from one cup.
Give one another of your bread but eat not from the
Same loaf.

Sing and dance together and be joyous, but let each
One of you be alone,
Even as the strings of a lute are alone though they
Quiver with the same music.

Give your hearts, but not into each other's keeping.
For only the hand of life can contain your hearts.
And stand together yet not too near together:
For the pillars of the temple stand apart,
And the oak tree and the cypress grow not in
Each other's shadow.[10]

Because men and women do not face the same economic and social compulsions to get or remain married today as they have in past decades, it is especially important that they begin their relationship as friends and build it on the basis of mutual respect. As people can no longer be forced into unchanging social or gender roles, or be forced to remain in unsatisfying relationships, "Love, honor and negotiate" have replaced older, more rigid rules. Furthermore, as individuals are now marrying later in life, with more life experiences, accepting each other's differences as well as similarities is vital. This acceptance must be a two-way street, based on *real* friendship and mutual respect.[11]

A relationship based on the shared cooperation of two well-grounded individuals presupposes a balance in shared responsibilities. Unlike a traditional gender-based relationship, where one of the partners may take on more responsibilities than would be considered healthy, responsibilities and tasks would, whenever possible, be allocated as evenly as possible. Communication is vital in such relationships, as partners would be able to comfortably express their feelings about taking responsibility in areas in which they are unaccustomed and ask for help, if necessary. Without healthy communication, both partners may become resentful or bitter, if they bottle up or suppress unspoken feelings; this could potentially lead to fear-based behaviors such as avoidance, denial, passive aggression, excessive need for control and addictive behaviors. A woman, for instance, would not need to feel isolated and abandoned with all childcare or housekeeping responsibilities, if she knew that she could ask her partner for help with some of these tasks. Conversely, a man who felt burdened with all of the breadwinning responsibilities could propose that his partner help as much as she is able in this area. In addition, frequent communication and negotiation between partners would increase each partner's understanding of the other's primary areas of responsibility.

The concept of shared partnership is undoubtedly strengthened today because two-earner couples are increasingly the norm. In contrast, in the 1960's, the majority of women relied on the incomes of their husbands to survive, since they couldn't find good paying jobs. Not only do young people today marry later in life, but when they do, they tend to marry for love. They want a fulfilling relationship: a best friend, a business partner, somebody to share sex, love and chores.[12]

In contrast to the dominant/non-dominant paradigm, a partnership model supports mutually respectful and caring relations. Because there is no need to maintain rigid rankings of control, there is also no built-in need for abuse. Partnership relations free our innate capacity to feel joy and to play. They enable us to grow mentally, emotionally and spiritually.[13] The values inherent in a partnership relationship, such as respect, dignity, appreciation, empathy, warmth, caring, open communication and caring only serve to increase self-esteem.[14]

Wholeness

Today it is widely accepted that men are not always domineering managers, nor are all women always passive caretakers. Gentle and sensitive men are expressing characteristics that are intrinsic to them; whereas logical and assertive women are doing the same for themselves. Although it's sometimes difficult for us to accept that men and women are capable of a broad range of behaviors associated with the other sex, by accessing and validating these qualities in ourselves as well as others, we can learn to appreciate our completeness and wholeness as members of the human family.[15]

An analogy to the concept of an individual's wholeness can be found in a children's book by Shel Silverstein entitled, *The Missing Piece Meets the Big O*. In the narrative, a missing piece, shaped like a piece of pie, searches in vain to find a "whole" pie, where it might fit and be taken along. It attempts to fit in to numerous "wholes," all of which are wrong for it for various reasons. When the piece finally finds a "whole," where it does fit, it eventually has to leave it, when it begins to grow and no longer "fits" into that whole as it once did. Continuing on its journey, the piece finds itself becoming curved and round, just like the whole pie it was seeking to fit in with. The story concludes as the new "whole" finds another like it, and they roll happily ever after down the road together, traveling along as two separate "wholes."[16]

Research shows that females who incorporate more "masculine" qualities along with their gender appropriate ones—have considerably higher self-esteem than those who are rated as exclusively "feminine." Conversely, men who incorporate more "feminine" traits actually have slightly higher self-esteem than do those who rate as exclusively "masculine. In terms of mental health for both men and women, just as was shown in Silverstein's story, wholeness has the edge. Studies of creativity make the same point: creative people have both higher than average self-esteem and higher than average degrees of androgyny.[17]

R. William Betcher and William S. Pollack discuss the changes that men need to make to create healthy relationships with themselves and with women:

Women have had the courage to show men their own true natures, but men are more reluctant to show women theirs. Much remains hidden under the swagger and bluster of insecurity and is unknown even to men, who are loath to renounce their dominant role in society. Such dominance not only victimizes the very women they care about, but places an unfair burden on men themselves. Men need to learn to understand their own inner reality—their thoughts, feelings, and fantasies, as well as the matrix of personal development from which they spring. Men need to be more aware, not just because women want them to, but for their own sake. The stereotypic male defense of not knowing what he feels, or of not giving it a sense of value because it "doesn't change anything," must be addressed in depth.[18]

In order to take part in an equal partnership, men must first learn is that this growth process will neither effeminize them, nor will it cause them to reject their masculine attributes. Rather, it is an expansion process that will provide them with more options and the capacity to respond more fully, honestly, humanly, and therefore, appropriately, to the demands of a situation.[19] Men's needs to prove themselves as men can create a never-ending, life-distorting chain that can drain their energies and will potentially destroy them. The ability of men to define their changes based on the knowledge of their own feelings and needs, rather than on the external demands of others is therefore vitally important.[20]

There are other specific changes than men need to make in order to be healthier: 1) They need to avoid women who are too submissive, easily dominated and dependent, and seek out women who relate to them equals. 2) They need to learn to experience passivity, (a counterpart to assertiveness training for women); as women begin to integrate their masculine sides, men should learn to integrate their feminine sides. 3) They need to postpone binding commitments (such as a premature marriage) which feel forced and unnatural. 4)

They need to recognize that their emotions are critical guides to reality. 6) They need to change themselves first before they try to change the world. 7) They need to remember that definitions of gender are always transitional and never static. 8) They need to support and insist on the continued growth and emergence of women. 9) They need to learn to ask for help when they need it. 10) They need to learn to cultivate friendships with other men. 11) They need to custom-make their own lives instead of relying on popularly-held ideas of what constitutes "normal" behavior. 12) They need to learn to repeat old patterns only if they feel natural and make sense to them.[21]

For men with greater authenticity and aliveness comes the opportunity to go beyond the state of arrested development, the perpetual adolescence that patriarchy can promote in grown men. It can be an opportunity to move away from unhealthy dependencies on women and toward healthy interdependencies, free of oppressive cultural baggage. Growing beyond patriarchal manhood means tolerating not being at the center of attention all of the time, but it also means not feeling that we must always appear to be in control, have an answer to every question or live life as continuous competition, especially with other men.[22]

In order for dominants to benefit from a more mutual relationship, they must recognize areas where they may unconsciously attempt to assert control with the non-dominants in their lives. In the case of dominant males, one of these methods is what Schaef calls the "pseudopodic" ego. Men's egos will often reach out, pull women (such as wives and secretaries) into their sphere, incorporate them and from that time on perceive that there is no difference between themselves and the women. Once a man "absorbs" a woman psychologically in this way, he literally does not perceive her as a separate being. Women who associate with men who ignore appropriate boundaries such as these often complain of being treated like one of their possessions. According to Schaef, this behavior is not entirely conscious on the man's part. Nevertheless, he can become angry and upset when the women tries to claim her rights to her own boundaries regarding her actions and possessions.[23]

Just as men learn to deal with their "manager" control issues, women must learn to stop playing the role of the gratuitous "mother," who compulsively gives to others as a primary way to gain validation and attention. Women need to reclaim their own positive power. For women genuine growth does not mean totally rejecting feminine needs and qualities such as dependency and nurturance; rather, it involves an expansion and development of the women's missing powerful side. Balance has to be maintained so that responses to men and others in their lives can be made fluidly and appropriately, rather than automatically and defensively.[24] Women need to clearly define their identities and preferences and ask for what they want directly, rather than indirectly. They need to deal with issues such as verbal assertiveness, setting boundaries, proactive decision-making and appropriate risk-taking. Finally women should be aware of any sexist expectations of their own, by recognizing how much they may measure their husband or significant other's worth by his economic success or status.[25]

As women stop creating primary relationships only with significant others, they are free to begin cultivating *a relationship with the self*. Taught to be perpetual "givers," many women never had a relationship with themselves, because they have been taught that to do so is selfish. Women must come to understand that self-awareness and focusing on the needs of the self are not the same as selfishness. The essence of self-awareness is a tenderness for and respect for the self which, in turn, allows one to be more tender and respectful toward others.[26]

Communication

One key area of change for women is in the area of communication. In order to be taken seriously in the workplace, many women have found that their accustomed style of being nice can be a powerful trap. When communicating with men in work settings, often women find that they rarely get attention by using feminine mannerisms such as smiling and waiting their turn. Although many men smile and nod during a conversation taking place in a business setting, they often register little of what is actually being said. Women can feel frustrated when this occurs.[27] When communicating with men in a business setting, women are advised to borrow techniques from male colleagues: 1) Sit at the middle of the conference table instead of sitting at the end. 2) Practice what you want to say in advance, especially your language and main points. This will give you the self-confidence to demand attention. 3) Communicate your central point hard, without conditions or apologies. 4) Don't end your statements tentatively or with a question mark. 4) Hone your listening skills. By actively listening you can be the one to take two or three ideas and clarify them. This will make it more difficult for a man to take your idea and "own" it later in the business meeting. For many women getting the job is only half the battle. The next step for a woman is to find her voice, as well as the power that goes with it.[28]

Women have become adept at reading both verbal and nonverbal emotional signals, while men have learned to minimize emotions having to do with vulnerability and hurt. In general, women come into a marriage groomed for the role of emotional manager, while men arrive with much less appreciation of the importance of this task for helping a relationship survive. For wives, intimacy means talking things over, especially about the relationship itself. Unfortunately, once married and as time goes on men, especially in more traditional relationships, spend less and less time talking with their wives.[29]

In addition, men can be somewhat slower in verbalizing problems and are less experienced when it comes to reading facial expressions of emotions than are women Even so, learning the skills necessary for a shared emotional intelligence is key to working out conflicts in marital relationships. Skills such as being able to calm down yourself and your partner, displaying empathy and listening well can help de-escalate marital conflicts and can make possible the healthy disagreements which can allow a marriage to flourish.[30]

Former non-dominants need to learn to take the risks and the responsibilities of communicating between equals without resorting to the methods of their (former) dominant partners. By contrast, dominants must learn to listen without interrupting and not try to take over the conversation, be dismissive, or raise their voices unnecessarily. Strategies such as not interrupting while the other person is talking or reflecting back to the other person what they've just stated could be employed to ensure that both parties are able to feel acknowledged, as well as able to express their respective points of view. Another method that has been widely endorsed is the use of "I feel" statements. By expressing a sentence such as, "I feel frustrated when you_____," the partner is merely making a statement about his or her feelings. Keeping statements at the feeling level often helps to lower feelings of defensiveness that the partner may experience during the confrontation.

In her book, *Emotional Freedom*, psychiatrist Judith Orloff offers some important advice for non-dominants in wishing to alter unhealthy patterns established with dominant individuals. Although it's important to assert oneself appropriately, Orloff advises to not try to control a controlling personality. Limits are set best, using a direct approach, which is caring or neutral. Throughout this process, one may have to remind the controller several times, always in a kind, respectful, but neutral tone. When explaining your point of view, remain calm, unapologetic, without becoming defensive. Orloff reminds non-dominants to be realistic and not expect miracles. After all, controllers are experts at controlling and will resist your attempts to redefine your relationship. Finally, Orloff advises that if you reach an impasse, agree to disagree, and make that subject off-limits.[31]

In my case, practicing healthy communication has helped me gradually move away from my former fear-based patterns. Timing has been important. If a conversation would not go particularly well on one occasion, I would try again on another, when emotions had cooled. As feeling safe is important for me, I've learned to practice my assertiveness skills over and over until they've felt "normal" to me. Finally, whenever possible, I try to remain calm and centered when trying out new strategies.

Because so much of what we do in relationships is based on unconscious, conditioned responses, those who wish to create a more equal relationship with their significant other might begin by simply expressing his or her desire to relate and behave more as an equal partner. This strategy could set the stage for more open and mutual communication. The focal point of discussions should center on concrete, observable behaviors. Although some will never be able to take personal feedback from their spouses, many can tolerate honest, sincere feedback which doesn't attack them personally, but instead deals with particular behaviors. They may not like this type of information, but they can tolerate it.[32] During this process it's important for partners to remain non-judgmental and not to assign blame, especially if they have been interacting in a codependent manner. It's worth remembering that both partners have each played their respective roles in response to conditioning, which are, to a large degree, automatic, and unconscious.[33] Fostering attitudes of patience and tolerance can help couples develop empathy with each other in their respective struggles to change their own dysfunctional patterns.

Interdependence

As mature adults we learn to make our way to the middle ground of interdependence, to the balance between dependence and independence which is characterized maturity and wholeness. . . Interdependence creates the authentic freedom of adulthood. It presupposes one's right to be dependent and independent at the same time. Such interdependence affirms your social nature by calling you to mutuality, equality and justice for everyone. Adults capable of interdependence honor themselves by taking responsibility for their own lives, while at the same time recognizing how others can contribute to it.[34]

Interdependence demands two separate, whole, autonomous people who do not need to protect themselves from each other. Interdependent couples can love one another for who he or she really is, not because of some false image; interdependent partners are friends. Partners can weave in and out of deep connection, are not always intimate with each other and can fight and argue with each other. Another name for interdependence is a *conscious, committed, cooperative relationship*. The following are some of the characteristics of an interdependent relationship: 1) an agreement that one of the main focuses of the relationship is healing and overcoming core issues stemming from destructive patterns learned in childhood; 2) a commitment to stay with conflicts until personal awareness and resolution occur; 3) a discovery process, where each partner's main intention is to discover and understand more about themselves and their partners, with the intention being not to change their partners; 4) a focus on each person's relationship with himself or herself, with the partners agreeing to support the other in this area; 5) a commitment to trusting yourself more, thereby protecting yourself from the possibility of being hurt by your partner. In instances such as these, if either party says or does something that unintentionally hurts the other, each can be trusted to ask for what he or she needs from the partner.[35]

Self-acceptance

As we develop self-acceptance, we can critically examine the role that conditional acceptance has had in our lives. Expressed in forms such as possible acceptance, partial acceptance and temporary acceptance, conditional acceptance is endemic in dominant/non-dominant relationships. Not only does it create in us the need to please others in neurotic and unhealthy ways, it creates a perpetual state of insecurity which forever denies us the self- acceptance and self-assurance that we crave. By its very nature conditional acceptance cannot make us feel fulfilled, peaceful or joyful.[36]

An alternative solution is to learn unconditional love and acceptance for ourselves and others. This attitude presumes that we're valid and acceptable no matter what we're like. The decision to live each day as if we are already accepted replaces our insecurity and striving with contentment and a sense of well-being. Unconditional acceptance gives us the grounding, freedom and joy we need to be whole and empowers us to use an accepting frame of reference as the center-point of our self-evaluation. Unconditional love drives the ability to accept oneself.[37] Learning to love and honor ourselves helps to pave the way to unconditional acceptance of others. When we learn to accept others unconditionally, they learn to behave more authentically with us.[38]

Expectations

What are our expectations from these changes? Will men stop being men and women stop being women? Will the feminine ideal of the loving but domesticated wife and mother, most often dependent on a man, gradually fade out of existence, only to be replaced by assertive, independent career-women? And what will happen to the male action hero endemic in our popular culture, the man who takes charge and saves the day through courage, critical thinking or physical prowess? Will he disappear, only to be replaced with another who is passive, insecure, overly sensitive, but always politically correct in his interactions?

In reality, neither the heroic male figure, nor the woman modeled after the feminine ideal is likely to disappear. These roles may, however, gradually lose their power over our behaviors, as we no longer feel compelled to conform to their rigid standards. Although previously considered based in biology, many gender-specific behaviors are now understood to be the result of learning. It's more likely that both men and women will play a wider variety of roles than they've played previously. As women continue to fill roles in the public arena, it will become increasingly difficult for the stereotyped gender roles to operate in *direct opposition* to each other, as they have in the past, e.g., fewer helpless female victims will mean that fewer masculine "heroes" will be needed to save them. As acceptable behaviors for males and females gradually become more open-ended, men and women will have to resort to other means to distinguish themselves, rather than these familiar but nonetheless polarizing roles.

In a departure from the women of previous generations, today's women are learning to become stronger and more positive advocates for themselves as well as for their children. By contrast, it has been found that men who have experienced raising children *do* change. As mentioned earlier in Chapter 4, one study found that single men and women care-givers were found to have almost identical levels of "feminine" traits.[39]

To increase flexibility with regard to our gender roles, we need to re-examine hidden assumptions and attitudes with regards to them. For instance, although mothers and other caretakers play a critical role in our society, these caring roles are not regarded highly in terms of remuneration or respect, as measured by social attitudes. Whereas, mothers from all backgrounds understand that this prejudice exists, regardless of their personal histories, they universally have problems accepting it. Whenever a mother experiences this type of prejudice, she should be free to speak up and ask the question, "Why?" Similarly, if a family member or associate judges a man's right to express grief or fear as "unmanly," he should have the right to question that assumption without fearing that by doing so he has jeopardized his status as a man. Hidden assumptions and prejudices such as these should not be accepted at face value, and "brushed over," but should be vigorously challenged and questioned.

Another of the "gender" blind spots of our culture is that we have a difficult time admitting what a wife can truly accomplish if she were to have an absent, ill or deceased husband. It's a poorly acknowledged fact that many women are quite capable of "picking up the pieces," in an intelligent and courageous manner in the event of the death or abandonment of a spouse. Although we are often accustomed to closing our eyes to a woman's strengths while her husband is alive, once he has died, paradoxically, it's *assumed* that she will be able to carry on, even if she is a single parent to a large family. Yet, despite the fact that, in times of war, famine and disaster, women and children have had to make do without men more often than not, our society still propagates the myth that women are the "weaker" sex.

A similar example of a "gender" blind-spot is the shame-based treatment that some men are subjected to when they are no longer able to function as breadwinners and must rely either on partner, wife, or some form of disability program for financial stability. These men are burdened enough dealing with their physical condition than to have to apologize or feel shame for their disability. Because of out-dated patriarchal norms, a man in this condition might be treated as less of a "man," not only by his male peers, but by women, as well. Nevertheless, simple logic dictates that no matter what the conditions of his illness or injury, a man before his illness or accident continues to remain a man after it.

Finally, those who challenge static and polarized gender roles attributed to women and men must learn to publicly commit to these changes. As overwhelming as it seems, change in the direction of partnership for each of us begins with small, baby steps, such as asking the "why" questions, previously mentioned. It's best to attempt small, humble and doable acts, rather than large, heroic and impossible ones. Another way to promote change is, whenever possible, to work with other people in teaching and/or discussion groups. We don't have to do anything earth-shaking to help change along. As powerful as patriarchy is, like all oppressive systems, it cannot stand the strain of lots of people doing something about it, beginning with the simplest act of speaking its name out loud. In addition, it's important to understand that emotional risks, such as the uncertainties of feeling lost, confused, scared and alone, as well as the potential of rejection, may accompany these changes.[40]

One simple, although powerful action toward change is when an individual courageously demands the right to live as a healthy and a whole person without apology. The fact that a person can be empowered in this way can have a tremendous effect on others. Without putting direct demands on others, it nevertheless sends a subtle but liberating message about *their* potential for growth. At the same time such individuals could represent role models to others still struggling with their transitions towards healthier behaviors. Repeated continuously by many persons over long periods of time, small incremental movements such as these can be deceptively powerful, presaging a gradual, but profound transformation in our society.

Elizabeth Ralston

Chapter 9

Implications for the Future

There are no guarantees that we will succeed in
freeing ourselves from the myths and structures
that still bind us to dysfunctional, painful, and
unjust ways of living . . . But even attempting
it is in itself an extraordinary adventure: . . .
And the more we dare to try out new paths, like
all explorers of new territory, the more we open
up further paths that make it possible for us to
experience life in ways we never thought possible.

Sacred Pleasure
By Riane Eisler

Some Observations

In taking stock of the rapid changes that have occurred over the past half century, it's clear that our norms governing gender relationships, while in a state of flux, nonetheless point the way towards increasing equality and balance and away from restriction and polarization. One of the main prerequisites in any healing process is to thoroughly examine the condition that is being healed; in this case, the conditions to be healed are learned behavior patterns which have contributed to gender-based codependency. As Gerda Lerner has pointed out, stepping outside of our traditional ways of thinking means being critical of all assumptions, values and definitions perceived as normal. Although her statement was directed mainly to women, her assertion that we can begin this process by trusting our trivialized or ignored experiences can be just as valid for men. The first step in this process would be to question our deep-seated resistance to accepting ourselves and our own knowledge as valid. Lerner concludes by saying that being critical of our conditioned ways of thinking means developing intellectual courage, the courage to stand alone, the courage to reach farther than our grasp and the courage to risk failure.[1]

Like many others, this critical thinking process has been difficult for me. Subjected to the same influences and constraints that have influenced so many others in maintaining the status quo, writing, and then speaking about these issues have aroused emotions in me which have fluctuated widely from joy and hope to anxiety and fear. Occasionally, I've experienced nostalgia for the way things used to be. More often, though, I've felt frustration and angst over a system which continues to question the notion of equality between men and women.

Despite my misgivings, I am convinced that the transition that we are experiencing is a liberating one. Although this change does not presage the end of "manly" men or "feminine" women, it does ask each of us to become more flexible in our concept of what it means to be a man or a woman; moreover, it demands an honesty from each of us which is both ruthless and courageous. Although initially intimating, becoming more honest in this way has made me feel increasingly empowered. Every time I've written or spoken about these issues, I've felt a little stronger and a little less afraid. Whereas in many instances I've felt mistrustful or cautious, there have been just as many where I've felt liberated and freed. It is the sort of discovery process that I ask my readers to experience for themselves.

Earlier in this book I described a pre-Judeo-Christian society which evidence suggests was peace-loving, equalitarian and cooperative. Although it's not possible to recreate this earlier society, we might revisit those elements we admire in it in an attempt to experience at least some of the lost gifts from these earlier times. We might want to begin by working towards the goal of peaceful coexistence, as well as developing the ability to work cooperatively with others: two apparent characteristics of these earlier societies.

Despite fitful stops and starts I believe that our society has increasingly sought ways to deal with conflicts through negotiation and cooperation, rather than through issuing ultimatums or resorting to warfare. I believe that, as the world becomes more complex, the conceptual framework of seeking peaceful resolution to conflicts will become increasingly significant in order to solve the many dire and pressing problems that confront us universally. These transitions appear to be occurring on two different levels.

The first is occurring at the level of the culture. There is a growing awareness that America, as well as other societies, is in need of an operating system that promotes a wider base of participation rather than relying on the exclusivity of a select few, a social structure where circles and communities of trust flourish, where collaboration replenishes our sense of security and direction, and where integrity grows from a larger sense of service to our shared progress.[2] An alternative system to the one that we now have would be based on an inclusive *power-with* partnership, where all voices have the right to be heard—not just the powerful voices of those in charge—and where all individuals have full membership in their communities—regardless their gender, race, religion, age, sexuality, or abilities.[3]

Power derived from domination and control over others has always been illusive. It's not surprising that Napoleon Bonaparte, considered to be one of the most adept leaders at military-style domination near the end of his life stated that, "Do you know what astonished me most in the world? The inability of force to create anything. In the long run, the sword is always beaten by the spirit."[4]

In an earlier chapter I suggested that an examination of our patriarchal culture should be important to recovering codependents. My primary concern in making this statement was meant to be deeper than the sole issue of male dominance in our society. As Allan Johnson has pointed out, "patriarchy isn't problematic because it emphasizes male dominance, but because it promotes dominance and control as ends in themselves." He adds that, ". . .all forms of oppression draw support from common roots, and whatever we do that draws attention to those roots undermines all forms of oppression."[5] As we gradually release the negative attributes of our present culture, such as the need for dominance and relationships based on hierarchy, we cannot know what types of social organization will come after. We can only hope that, as we consciously change our attitudes and behaviors, a shift will occur in the direction of cooperation and equalitarianism.

The second transition is occurring at the level of the individual, where women and men strive to become more fully human. My hope is that throughout the individual recovery process, we will increasingly be able to acknowledge the humanity that we have in common, regardless of our gender. I admit that I have personal reasons for wanting this process to continue. I view the dominator ethic as a failed system which has led to multi-generational misery, where cruel and harsh practices have been the norm. In such a system, not only subordinates, but dominators are victims. This fact was evident to me, when I learned that perpetrators in my own family had been victimized as children. Acknowledging patterns such as these can prevent us from demonizing others needlessly, and can create in us a greater awareness of the *system* ultimately responsible for our dominant/subordinate relationship patterns.

In numerous ways women and men are learning to appreciate and nurture loving and trusting relationships, within as well as across gender lines. Despite our culture's tendency to model unhealthy or dysfunctional behaviors in the name of love, countless individuals are consciously choosing healthier ways of relating to one another. In the process they are deliberately trying to unlearn and relearn how to love.[6] Some are accomplishing this through individual, family and/or group therapies. Others engage in self-help groups which range from women and men's support groups and workshops to a variety of twelve-step recovery groups, where individuals learn not only healthier ways of relating to each other, but learn to be more loving to themselves, through nurturing and accepting their own "inner child."[7]

At Home

John is the primary caregiver for his wife, Anna, who suffers from dementia. Marsha is a successful executive for a major corporation. Married for five years, Tom and Eva are owners of a neighborhood restaurant. With stops and starts our concepts of "maleness" and "femaleness" are being redefined. Although men and women continue to play roles typical of their own sex, our concepts of appropriate roles for males or females will continue to broaden to include at least some roles which, until recently, were considered atypical of that sex.

In a 2009, nationwide study of over three thousand couples sponsored the Rockefeller Foundation in conjunction with *TIME,* it was found that virtually all partners polled reported that they frequently engage in re-negotiating the rules of their relationships, work and family. Maria Shriver, one of the study's authors, found that an overwhelming majority of men and women reported sitting down at their kitchen tables to coordinate their family's schedules, duties and responsibilities, including child care and elder care, at lease two to three times per week.[8]

The extraordinarily rapid changes, especially in the area of work, where women are now fifty percent of the workforce, have been difficult for many to keep up with. As one man interviewed stated, "All of us grew up thinking this was a man's world, that doors were just going open to us because we had a Y chromosome . . . And suddenly, we have to adjust to the fact that that's not the case. And the recession has made it even more intense for us. . . It's more like we're finally, for the first time, in a position where it's no longer only a man's world."[9]

Elizabeth Ralston

According to sociologist Michael Kimmel, although some men have harshly protested and others attempt to downgrade women's progress and achievements, most American men simply continue to go about their lives, falling somewhere between eager embrace and resigned acceptance of women's equality.[10] Kimmel adds that this change in the attitude of males may be based in part because men sense that, as a society, we've reached a point of no return. Women are now in the labor force as well as almost all other public arenas, to stay.[11]

The largest, if least acknowledged, response to women's equality is the quiet acceptance of gender equality on the part of men at both the public and private levels. In the public sphere, the majority of American men support wage equality, comparable worth and women's candidacies for public office. Surveys consistently show "substantial and persistent" long-term trends toward increasing endorsement of gender equality in families. With only minor changes in attitude, most American men have adapted to the dual-career model, now typical of most marriages.[12] Most men have not discarded their traditional ideas of masculinity with this acceptance. Although partially grounded in financial need, their attitude change also seems to have resulted because of an increased awareness of the importance of wage equality for women as well as a growing lack of acceptance for discrimination, bullying and harassment. Lastly, men have gradually and without struggle have drifted into more egalitarian relationships because they care about and love their wives, partners and children.[13]

The "traditional" family, where the father works and the mother remains at home, today comprises fewer than 20 percent of American families; it's easy to forget that only sixty years ago, this pattern was considered the norm. By the mid-1990's, however, close to 60 percent of all married couples were dual-earners. This has had tremendous implications for the future of the family, as well as for our social institutions.[14] In a study of 300 dual-earner couples, researchers Barnett and Rivers found that families are thriving in the dual-earner version. The family these couples create is one in which the quality of life of all its members has improved: they're happier, healthier and more well-grounded than family members of the 1950's.[15]

As previously mentioned, when women entered the workforce, they took on the bulk of the domestic tasks thought of as the "second shift." Although women still spend more time in domestic tasks relative to men, it appears that over the past forty years, the trend has gradually shifted, so that men have been taking on more domestic responsibilities. Research from Oxford University quoted in a recent news magazine article indicated that between 1965 and 2003, college educated men performed 33 percent more housework than they had before, and men who never completed high school did a remarkable 100 percent more housework. Family research prepared by the Council on Contemporary Families shows a similar change in male behavior in the area of child-care. The research showed that fathers under the age of 29 spend an average of 4.3 hours per work day with their children, almost double that of men in the same age range studied in 1977. For perhaps the first time recorded, married men complain of difficulties in maintaining a balance between work and home life. In 2008, 59 percent of employed fathers in dual-earner families in a University of California study complained of suffering work-family conflict, up from 35 percent in 1977. By contrast, the number of women who reported similar conflicts increased by only 5 percent, to 45 percent. One of the conclusions of the research was that norms have now shifted so that taking care of a child is now considered an intrinsic part of what it means to be a father.[16]

According to historian Stephanie Coontz, contrary to popular wisdom, women's entrance into the work force has been positively correlated with a lower divorce rate. From a peak of 22.8 divorces per 1,000 couples in 1979, the divorce rate dropped to 16.7 divorces per 1,000 married couples by 2005; those more recently married seem to be following the trend. Today, divorce rates tend to be highest in states where fewer wives have paid jobs and lowest in states where more than 70 percent of married women work outside the home.[17] Those men whose attitudes have become increasingly egalitarian during the course of their marriage report higher marital satisfaction, as do their wives. It's possible that these factors have created an environment where more men are beginning to accept, and even embrace women's equality.[18] Whatever the causes, more marriages are lasting in each new generation of newlyweds since the baby boomers, and these marriages are fairer, more intimate and more respectful than couples from previous eras would have ever dared to dream.[19]

In a 2005 study of 50 dual earner couples, 12, or close to 25 percent, were defined as post gender, where the couples assumed that all tasks were shared and appeared to have consciously moved beyond gender as a mechanism for organizing their relationships. Post gender mothers and fathers assumed that responsibility for children was shared, and post gender fathers saw themselves as responsible for childcare tasks, and sought to be open to learning new skills necessary in helping their wives with childcare tasks.[20]

According to a 2007 article, in the previous decade, the number of stay-at-home dads has tripled. It was reported that, as fathers today put much more of a focus on nurturing and caring for their kids than on the traditional breadwinner role, the number of men as well as woman suing their employers for family leave has soared. Men make up a growing segment of this group—11 percent, compared with 5 percent a decade ago. Out of 600 dads surveyed by the Minnesota's Department for Families and Children's Services, a majority said that the most important role was to "show love and affection" to kids. "Safety and protection" came next, "moral guidance," "taking time to play" and "teaching and encouraging." The men surveyed put "financial care" last on their list.[21] Although these reports show a vast improvement over the parental participation of previous generations, women still put in roughly twice as much time as men in child care responsibilities.[22]

According to sociologist Michael Kimmel, when men do share housework as well as childcare, the payoff at home is significant. Recent research has shown that when men increase their share of housework and child care, their children are happier, healthier and do better in school. They are less likely to be diagnosed with ADHD, less likely to be put on prescription medications, and less likely to see a child psychologist for behavioral problems. They also have lower rates of absenteeism and high school achievement scores.[23]

Studies have shown that men who do help with domestic responsibilities are healthier, smoke less, drink less and take recreational drugs less often. They are more likely to stay in shape and more likely to go to doctors for routine screenings, but are less likely to use emergency rooms or miss work due to illness. These men are also psychological healthier than

Elizabeth Ralston

men who are not involved in housework or childcare. They are less often diagnosed with depression, see therapists and take prescription medication less often compared to men who do not share housework. These men report higher level of marital satisfaction, live longer, and have more sex.[24]

Lastly, wives of egalitarian husbands, regardless of class or race and ethnicity, report the highest levels of marital satisfaction and lowest rates of depression, and are less likely to see therapists or take prescription medication. They are also more likely to stay fit, perhaps because they have more leisure time.[25]

At Work

In our country the corporate structure has traditionally been organized like a pyramid, with control ranked hierarchically. Business experience today shows that this model can stifle productivity and creativity. The large, hierarchic corporation frequently lacks flexibility and responsiveness; it becomes set in its ways, riddled with pecking order politics, and closed to new ideas or outside influences.[26]

Mary Parker Follett, a virtually unknown Wellesley College graduate, first introduced the concept of sharing power in the workplace in 1924. Follett's model emphasized the value of interconnectedness and collaboration, a radical departure from traditional practices of the time.[27] Throughout the years, Follett's theme has been successfully replicated in management literature, and was integral to the successful Japanese business model after World War II.[28]

Organizations developed from a partnership model have common characteristics. Their hierarchies are flatter and less rigid, which, where they do exist, become "hierarchies of actualization" that encourage innovation, flexibility and individual initiative. Leadership shifts from a model of command and control to one based on a supportive web of relationships that encourage dialogue and problem-solving.[29] Power shifts from the coercive use of manipulations to the development of generative, power-sharing relationships that enable groups to easily work together to solve problems.[30] Communication and teamwork are valued, taught and modeled by group leaders. The type of communication modeled by leaders is open and forthright.[31]

Dove-tailing with this new model, the concept of emotional intelligence has altered our expectations for managers. Managers are expected to be increasingly skilled in basic emotional abilities, such as being attuned to the feelings of those one works with, being able to handle disagreements so that they don't escalate, and having the ability to get into flow states while working. Under this new model leadership is not viewed as an act of domination, but as the art of persuading others to work toward common goals.[32]

Managers skilled in the older, more traditional model may often develop adversarial relationships with staff line workers. Although they are willing to criticize, they are slow to give praise; this attitude leaves employees with the impression that from management's perspective, their errors have made a bigger impression than their abilities. Increasingly, today's managers are encouraged to give balanced critiques that focuses on the positive as well as negative aspects of the job, as well as what needs to be accomplished in order to improve.[33]

Some of the factors defining emotional intelligence are self-awareness, self-regulation, which would include the individual being reasonably in control of feelings and impulses, good judgment and fair-mindedness, motivation,

Elizabeth Ralston

empathy, and social skills, where the individual has the ability to manage relationships.[34]

In a ten year psychological study managers from several companies were asked to identify areas of competency that typified their organization's outstanding leaders. When the ratio of technical skills, IQ and emotional intelligence were measured as factors contributing to excellence in performance, emotional intelligence proved to be twice as important as the others for jobs at all levels. The managers determined that this attribute played an increasingly important role, especially at the highest levels of management.

Other studies had similar findings. In a 1996 company-wide study senior managers who demonstrated significant amounts of emotional intelligence helped their divisions outperform yearly earnings goals by 20%. Divisions under managers who showed lesser amounts of emotional intelligence under-performed by almost the same amount.[35]

Although the majority of American corporations continue to follow the older model, in many companies today the emphasis is increasingly being placed on collaboration and adaptability; learning on the run is valued rather than the process that occurs in the traditional system, where employees are placed on the defensive for making mistakes and therefore fail to learn from them. This process encourages employees to look forward rather than backward, to take a joyful rather than a grim attitude.[36]

A New Reality

In contrast to women, the expectations of men, especially in the area of career, have remained much the same as those of past eras. Despite this fact, as men's jobs in the construction and manufacturing sectors have continued to shrink due to automation and outsourcing, men will have to compete for fewer and fewer jobs considered by many to be appropriately "masculine." Of the 15.3 million new jobs projected to be created over the next decade, the vast majority will occur in fields that are now dominated by women. Of the twelve job titles expected to grow the most in the upcoming decade, only two, accountant and construction worker are male-dominated. The rest, such as teachers, registered nurses and customer service representatives, remain dominated predominantly by women. As more "manly" occupations continue to migrate oversees or are eliminated because of economic downturns, the percentage of recent male high school and college graduates who are chronically unemployed has increased to 20.5 percent, three points higher than the rate of their female counterparts.[37]

In order for men to take part in the economic life of the future, they will need to stop limiting themselves to the narrow range of "acceptable" masculine positions and take advantage of the anticipated employment growth in the service sectors of our economy expected to occur over the next decade. Instead of looking for jobs in the shrinking pool of masculine jobs, some should begin to look for jobs in service sectors, such as in the teaching or nursing professions. In order to take part in these changes, men today would do well to accept an expanded notion of manhood that is nurturing as well as masculine. The changes in some professions are already taking place. The percentage of men who are nurses, for instance, has doubled over the past twenty-five years.[38]

As we adjust to dual-earner partnership as the new "normal," finding creative ways to allow men and women to integrate, combine and sometimes alternate their responsibilities to work and to family could be the single more effective "pro-marriage" program of the 21st century. Now that women have so many more options outside marriage and men have more balanced authority within it, the following changes should be considered, especially by our business and government sectors:

1. Given the fact that women are likely to remain in the workforce, enhancing gender equality will reduce, not increase tensions between men and women.
2. Creating laws and institutions such as increased parental leave and flex time that will encourage mothers and fathers to participate more easily in childcare. This will enable fathers, especially, not only to participate actively as parents within viable marriages, but to remain in contact with their children in the event of divorce.
3. Embracing flexible working hours, family leave, child care and time for care of elders to enable married couples and other individuals with care-giving obligations to balance the demands of work and family equitably.[39]

There are many areas of transition ahead for all of us that will require a combination of faith, self-examination and open, candid communication. Women must face the ways in which they take on too much of the burden of housework and then resent their partners for it. Men should learn to grow comfortable leaving work meetings early for family obligations and being transparent about it with their colleagues. Employers should try out policies that acknowledge their workers as whole human beings.[40]

Changes in the World

At the United Nations Conference on Women in 1995, Hillary Clinton made a profound statement deceptive in its simplicity: "Human rights are women's rights, and women's rights are human rights for one and for all." Her assertion was seen by many as presaging a shift in U. S. policy which focused on the concept that the way for nations to prosper was to pay attention to women's rights, concerns and welfare.[41]

Increases in women's participation in foreign governments have contributed to positive changes in women's status and rights in these countries. Women now hold at least 30 percent of the seats in parliaments of seventeen countries, including nine European countries and twenty-two women are speakers of parliaments.[42] In recent years women have been elected heads of state in countries such as Germany, Denmark, Canada, Ireland, Finland, Lithuania, the Philippines, Chile, Argentina, Brazil, Australia, New Zealand, Iceland, South Korea, Thailand, Bangladesh, Liberia and Malawi. Almost half of the Swedish parliament are women, as is half of the Swedish cabinet.[43] The same phenomenon has occurred in African countries such as Liberia, Malawi and Rwanda, where 48 percent of the legislature are now women. Decades ago, Women leaders such as Indira Ghandi of India, Margaret Thatcher of Great Britain and Golda Meier of Israel first began this trend by being elected prime ministers in their respective countries. In recent years the influence of Christine Lagarde, head of the IMF, and Hillary Rodham Clinton, former U. S. Secretary of State has helped to raise the international profile of women.

Increasingly, both government and non-government leaders in developing countries are becoming aware of the benefits that accompany increased education for girls. The non-profit Central Asia Institute has spent over a decade building and funding schools primarily for girls in Northern Pakistan and Afghanistan. Its philosophy is that the best way to promote peace in these troubled areas is to provide an education for its children, and that an entire culture can be changed by helping its girls become educated so they can help themselves.[44]

As part of increased international efforts towards improving conditions for women, the Grameen Bank of Bangladesh, created in 1976 to provide micro-loans for low-income individuals to work their way out of poverty. To date, the bank has 2.3 million borrowers, most of whom are women. The decision to lend to women instead of to men was pragmatic, as women have demonstrated more responsibility in using the money to build small businesses to support themselves and their families than have men. Despite a 78% illiteracy rate, Bangladesh has seen a marked increase in economic gains since the program was initiated. The bank's micro-lending model has since expanded to many other developing and industrialized countries, including the United States.[45]

In a similar vein, La Pietra Coalition, an alliance of corporations, nonprofits and governments, has recently been established to make women partners at all levels in the global economy. Its plan is to enable roughly one billion women to become members of the global economy by 2025.[46]

It's not surprising that nations considered more partnership-oriented demonstrate increasing equality in relationships between men and women. Scandinavian nations, for example, provide at least some support for child-care. As reflected in their governments' subsidies to all parents, including single mothers, Scandinavian nations demonstrate the degree to which they value care-giving economically. Unlike in our country, where welfare recipients are often viewed with contempt, welfare does not carry a social stigma in Scandinavian countries.[47] In addition, in Sweden, where women's salaries on average make up 39 percent of the household income (considered the highest percentage in the world), men also help more with housework and childcare in comparison with those in other countries.[48]

In 1995 Swedish legislation helped to change public perception of the appropriate parenting role for men. In this landmark decision, couples were told that they would lose one month of paid parental leave unless the father took it. Today, up to eighty percent of Swedish fathers take up to four months of paid parental leave, up from 4 percent only ten years ago. In Swedish society today the perception is that men are expected to be competent in child-rearing, and are expected to spend time at home with their children. Thus, legislation and public policy helped Swedish men to embrace their roles as fathers in a more holistic fashion.[49]

A Case for Spirituality

All of our major faiths share the core values of sensitivity, empathy, caring and nonviolence. We can use these values to develop a partnership spirituality that infuses our lives with empathy, caring and responsibility—a spirituality that focuses on joy, life and love and establishes a moral standard which calls each of us to approach our lives with awareness, empathy and respect. This standard fosters the sense of oneness that is the core of partnership spirituality.[50] Partnership spirituality recognizes that when people are truly loved rather than abused they are more likely to be empathic, caring and creative, qualities that enable individuals to develop compassionate spiritual qualities. Many from both established religions, as well as New Age groups, are leading the way toward establishing this type of ethic.[51]

As many entering twelve-step recovery programs have rejected the religion of their childhoods, participants are encouraged to seek connection with a higher power of their own understanding. It is for this reason that members of these groups are discouraged from passively accepting unhealthy messages from any religious group and are encouraged to experience their own individual sense of spirituality, either through prayer and meditation and/or by seeking out religious or spiritual organizations that offer them a balanced and nourishing message.

Relationships Revisited

One who strives to develop healthy relationships gradually develops the emotional wholeness to relate to another in a collaborative, cooperative manner in a relationship based upon a healthy interdependence between equals. Although partners may designate one or the other to lead in particular areas in the relationship, this leadership role should be based upon who has strengths and/or talents in a given area. The decision should not be arbitrarily based on a preconceived power structure. In addition, partners should be able to acknowledge the importance of tasks required of the other, regardless of how seemingly ordinary those tasks may seem.

In seeking out partnership roles, increasingly, women and men are transcending the restricting patterns of gender stereotypes. In contrast to the extremely masculine person, characterized as domineering, angry, arrogant, out of touch with his own feelings and unwilling to show weakness, or the extremely feminine person, characterized by terms such as is victimized, feels depressed, knows nothing, is unwilling to show strength and feels inferior, a "whole" person has been characterized as creative, relaxed, curious, attentive, draws self-wisdom from feelings, is flexible and feels equal. When the choice is clear, regardless of one's gender, who wouldn't say yes to owning the characteristics of the "whole" self just described?[52]

Individuals taking part in interdependent relationships are committed in new ways that differ from codependent relationships. The commitment is not just to the other person, but also to oneself, where the personal and spiritual growth of each individual is of paramount importance. In interdependent relationships the commitment is not to the *form* but to the *process,* while the emphasis on partnership supports the move toward co-creation and service for committed couples.[53]

Full Circle

While writing this book, I've witnessed numerous changes of historic proportions. Some of them have been so gradual that I don't remember when I first became aware of them. Was it when I first noticed the large numbers of young men pushing children in strollers in the park? Or perhaps it was when I learned that Australia, coming from a conservative tradition regarding women's rights, had just elected its first woman prime minister. Or, was it decades ago when I first began to notice women's voices reporting the news on the radio? Or was it when I began to notice increasing numbers of women representatives in the U.S. Congress. Over the years there have been countless examples from increasing numbers of women Supreme Court Justices to police officers, to medical doctors and highway maintenance workers, to the growing numbers of women artists and musicians. Or perhaps it began when I first met a young man who chose to be a stay-at-home dad for his infant daughter. Or was it when my own mother, who had been out of the work force for most of her adult life, discovered the joy of earning her first paycheck in forty years at the age of 62. Although understated and underreported, these changes, quietly and inexorable as drops of rain, have nevertheless produced steady but potent erosions in the reality that we have always known. Every deviation from the "norm" of gender stereotypes has quietly hammered a nail in the coffin of the status quo, and has contributed to our shift in values towards increasing equality between men and women.

As far as my recovery is concerned, I have made vast improvements in some areas, while still feeling challenged by others. Increasingly, I have felt empowered to ask for my needs to be met from others. I am less sensitive or concerned with other's opinions of me. I fear failure less, and am able to focus more on those behaviors that help me to succeed. I've adopted a more optimistic view of my abilities. I've become more assertive and more of a risk taker. I am less susceptible to others who seek to control me, either overtly or covertly. Because of my growing awareness of the *systemic* factors in our social institutions which have contributed to my codependency, I've found myself better able to detach from those individuals who have mistreated me either because of my gender, or because of my role as a non-dominant. Most importantly, I've increasingly been able to perceive myself as a person who happens to be a woman, instead of its opposite, a woman who struggles to be a person.

In some situations I still feel challenged, however. In the presence of verbally assertive individuals, most often men, I sometimes feel compelled to remain silent, unable to interrupt or break the flow of the conversation. At times I still have a difficult time perceiving myself consistently as at the center of my own world, and not a satellite of another's. Occasionally, I still find myself judging myself by others' standards, rather than my own. I sometimes question my right to assert myself. However difficult it may be for me to make the changes necessary, I remain fully committed to making them, as I understand that I must continue this process in order to make my way in the world.

In my search for healthy role models, I've been increasingly attracted to the popular heroic figure. Empowered to act alone in the world, often against overwhelming odds, the heroic figure is depicted as a paragon of success, especially when he/she is confronted with opposing negative forces of immense strength. Although taken mostly from comic books and arguably a two-dimensional prototype, popular heroic models have provided me with simple straight-forward concepts that have helped me to envision success. I admire their forthrightness, their unabashed sense of self-confidence, their strength, fortitude and their ability, without a second thought, to take action on their own or another's behalf. If they fail, heroes keep on trying until they *do* succeed. My ability to identify with heroes has been a tremendous antidote in my recovery process.

It's an unfortunate commentary on the state of our gender relations, however, that our heroic figures have traditionally been almost exclusively male. Although they have provided young boys and men with generations of positive role models, heroic male figures have unfortunately accomplished this feat at the expense of the psychological health of just as many generations of girls and women, who have often been depicted, in relationship to them, as weak, dependent or victimized. I find it ironic that, without exception, the female heroic models that do exist have invariably been depicted as feminists. This fact has underscored my belief that although our society's heroic model of success has traditionally been rooted in the male hero, women should unashamedly borrow from it to help themselves in their efforts to achieve their personal goals.

Fortunately, our popular views have been rapidly changing along these lines, as demonstrated by the increasing number of movies and T.V. shows depicting strong female heroines that are currently being produced. Images such as these can help women develop a sense of empowerment in approaching their life's challenges, whether or not they are consciously aware of this fact. From Wonder Woman to Zena, Warrior Princess, the popular hero is now also female.

I feel deeply appreciative of the efforts of the women and men I've come in contact with in recent years who have dealt with and continue to deal with each other every day in a spirit of partnership and collaboration. For these individuals cooperative relationships are proving a safe, sane and healthy way to interact with others. Their examples have been an inspiration for me, and I've experienced deep humility as I've learned from them. The important message in observing their efforts is that they are not behaving as partners because they feel guilty or want to please; they are behaving as partners because that is what they really want to do. I am awed and amazed by their collective efforts. The instances of men, in particular, have left me eager to witness more of the same going forward, and their remarkable examples have led me to believe that perhaps true partnership between women and men will one day become our new "normal."

So, how, then, do we deal with the problem of gender inequality? A good place to start would be to have the courage to admit its existence. We won't end these problems by pretending that they don't exist or that we don't have to deal with them. Neither can members of one gender be asked to "own" the problem, as imbalances belong to both sexes. By denying that this type of inequality and oppression doesn't exist, we must deny the reality of our own experience and its consequences for people's lives, including our own.[54] As men and women have always lived and worked together in social communities, it's often difficult to find the truth of gender inequities in our system. Men have always been born to and, for the most part, raised by women, and women's lives have always been bound up with those of men, whether they be fathers, husbands, brothers or sons. Intimacy between the genders has always been a central part of human experience; all of these things can make it difficult to see that gender oppression exists, much less how it works.[55]

And yet, it's important that we not only try to see when it exists, but also to notice how it works. Change comes about when we become conscious of what has been unconscious and understand that learned responses, no matter how seemingly entrenched, can be unlearned as well. It's precisely because women and men are involved in each other's lives that they must learn to treat one another in a caring and loving manner, while still being true to themselves and their own ideals. Although many in my parents' generation may not have been able to achieve this, those of us that have come after them are learning, gradually, to treat one another from a spirit of empathy and good will, while at the same time showing honesty and courage in our communications with one another.

The first truth that I've come to understand is that as members of the human race, both women and men are fully functioning as human beings, who, as such, should be able to access their inner resource of strength and guidance regardless of whether or not this strength and guidance comes from their male or female sides. The second truth that I've learned is that countless individuals are now involved in this process of change. Collectively, as we let go of the straight jackets that bind us to restrictive gender roles, we will be free to seek healthier ways of living, ways that are the inevitable expressions of our true natures.

Afterward

Many changes have occurred since *The Mother and the Manager* was first published in December of 2014. In 2016 and then again in 2020 our country experienced two monumental and norm-shattering presidential elections, the ramifications of which we are still grappling with today. As a country, we still struggle from the aftermath of a global pandemic, extreme political division, an epidemic of gun violence and the worsening effects of global warming. Internationally, many nations are struggling to create or maintain workable governments based on democratic principles, free from autocratic norms and corruption.

These dramatic events may seem detached and distant from the endeavors of our personal lives, where so many of us seek to establish caring, workable relationships based on the principles of partnership and equality. And yet, after perusing the news headlines each day I wonder how separated our private and public experiences really are. I suspect that in some mysterious way, they may be inextricably linked. When I stop to think of the connection between our public and private attitudes about issues such as mutual respect, the quest for workable problem-solving based on cooperative efforts and the efforts for equality with others, I struggle with the implicit, yet strangely elusive relationship between the two.

Increasingly, I've come to suspect that our close, sometimes intimate relationships are a mirror, almost a microcosm of these much larger struggles. If our close relationships can be perceived as representative of a larger whole, then the essential question remains the same in all of these domains, no matter the scope or size of them. How can we as humans best relate to one another, through fear, control or manipulation, or by reaching out to cooperate, collaborate and co-exist with one another on an equal basis?

It is within this context that I've emphasized the importance of viewing our relationships with others through a cultural and historical lens to more completely understand how we as social beings have learned to negotiate our personal relationships based on understandings passed down from previous generations. Regardless of the strength of our inherited traditions on our current behaviors, however, the rapid-fire cultural changes which have occurred over the past half century have increasingly pointed towards creating a foundation of equalitarianism in the way that we relate to others, especially those in our family and friendship circles. As a culture we appear to be moving away from close relationships dominated by hierarchy. Whether dealing with the larger issue of planetary co-existence, or with the more intimate one of working relationships between individuals and small groups, it appears that a collaborative, cooperative ethic based on equality is optimal for our personal as well as our collective survival as human beings who share our planet with billions of other human beings, as well as with a vast array of other living creatures.

Cultural Changes

There have been multiple stops and starts on our collective journey towards a more equitable society. In the U.S. numerous changes have occurred quite rapidly without much fanfare. African Americans and people of color are increasingly visible in local, state-wide and national leadership positions in our country, from Supreme Court Justices, leadership positions at the Pentagon, mayors of large and small cities, members of national and statewide congresses, district attorneys and heads of police departments, to name just a few; they have also become increasingly visible in our religious, legal and scientific communities. Efforts continue towards gender equity. Currently, the U.S. has twelve female governors in states across the country. Half of our current administration's cabinet members are female, as is the current head of the U.S. Federal Trade Commission, the CDC and our current Vice President, Kamala Harris. Women are increasingly being elected or appointed to local government positions such as mayors and police commissioners, to federal judgeships, as well as justices and chief justices of state supreme courts; in addition, the number of women U.S. congressmen and senators continues to steadily rise. Our third female U. S. Supreme Court Justice was recently appointed. Our director of national intelligence and the head of the CIA are currently women. The inclusion of numbers of women and people of color of this magnitude in our national and regional leadership would have been unthinkable even two decades ago.

Changes toward increasing gender equity are taking place in other areas in our culture. Women on the U. S. Women's Soccer Team recently defied the odds against gender equality as they sued the American Soccer Federation and won for equal wages and pay as the members of the Men's team. Despite having won The Women's World Cup three times in the past decade, the women were paid only a small percentage of what the men, who had never won a World Cup, were paid. The members of the women's team persisted in their lawsuit and won. Unable to change the unequal wage disparities handed down by the World Soccer Federation, the Men's Team agreed, with the support of its players, to split their wages equally with the women's team.[1] Our traditional cultural norms are changing in other areas, as well. In a suburban area south of Omaha, Nebraska, a large number of female police officers were recently hired by the local chief of police. This appeared to be part of a deliberate strategy to reduce the likelihood of misconduct and excess violence in the force, traditionally composed mostly of men. The chief, a former Iowa state trooper, believes both from research and his own experience that diversity not only makes for better policing, it reduces the use of force against civilians. Research has also shown that when female officers are used, citizen complaints have decreased in situations where interactions have been potentially volatile. Research has also shown that female officers can excel at de-escalation in potentially volatile situations and consequently have to use force less often than do male officers.[2]

Nevertheless, events that played out during the 2016 presidential election demonstrate continuing concerns regarding gender equity that still challenge us as a society. The campaign between candidates Donald Trump, Republican, and Hillary Clinton, Democrat, was a hugely consequential event in our nation's history, as Mrs. Clinton was our nation's first female nominee for U.S. president. The competition also demonstrated the differential treatment that as a culture we continue to tolerate for men towards women in comparison to the treatment that we expect women to give to men. Throughout the campaign, Mr. Trump almost obsessively referred to Mrs. Clinton as dishonest, dangerous and corrupt. On numerous occasions the Republican and his supporters would repeatedly chant the phrase, "Lock her up." The ostensible cause for this chant was Mrs. Clinton's use of a private e-mail account for her government business while Secretary of State. While the FBI considered Mrs. Clinton's e-mail use to be an unwise action, it did not judge it to be an indictable offense.

Another example of Mr. Trump's disrespect towards Mrs. Clinton occurred during their one televised debate, which took place in a town-hall setting. While Mrs. Clinton spoke, Mr. Trump glared at her, looming from behind her in an ominous manner. While he spoke, Mrs. Clinton did not respond to Mr. Trump in a similarly disrespectful manner.

Although Mrs. Clinton was critical of Mr. Trump during her speeches, often stating that she believed that he was not qualified to be president, she never demonstrated the persistent attitude of disrespect towards him that he did towards her in either her speeches or public appearances. The vast difference between the treatment given to Mrs. Clinton by Mr. Trump, in comparison to that accorded to him by her throughout the 2016 campaign speaks volumes about how our society continues to tolerate blatant disrespect towards a woman by a man, even though this same type of treatment would not be considered appropriate if reciprocated towards a man by a woman, even in such a high profile competition such as a presidential election.

Throughout the 2020 and 2022 election cycles a partisan divide dominated the philosophical landscape between those who lean toward democratic values and those who follow a more conservative world view. Many of these conflicts have centered about the issue of control, who has control and how that control should be exercised; basic questions have been raised as to how much control are we as individuals able to have over ourselves and our own lives, and how much we can have control over the lives of others. Among the many areas of dispute are the issues of immigration, as well as racial and gender equality. The schism between these radically different world views has only seemed to deepen over time. Many of us have naturally related these issues of control to how they might affect us in our personal quests for healthy relationships with important persons in our lives.

And yet, our collective impetus towards equality continues. Women are increasingly playing prominent leadership roles on the international stage, such as Ursula Van der Leyden, the current European Commission President. In 2022, women were chosen to lead as Prime Ministers for the countries of Sweden and Finland. These changes have been extremely rapid and yet they have been treated as almost routine by the media. In the Nordic country of Finland, national awareness is being fostered of the importance of partnership between the genders.[3] Iceland is another northern country where partnership values are becoming increasingly normalized.[4]

Many in less equalitarian countries unfortunately continue to struggle against oppression, however. Nobel Peace Prize winner Maria Messa of the Philippines has been incarcerated many times for speaking out against the autocratic leadership of its last president.[5] In Iran women and men continue to engaging in grass roots protests against arbitrary restrictions of women demanded by the government. The opposition to the autocratic Russian regime continues, despite the incarceration and murder attempts of opposition leaders, as well as the war waged against the democratic government of Ukraine. These examples of courageous individuals struggling against their autocratic governments suggest to me that there must be something intrinsic in the human condition that seeks freedom from unjust and unreasonable controls.

Emotional Challenges

In the area of personal relationships in the U.S., both men and women are experiencing important changes. Increasingly, however, it is women who have taken the lead in asking that their emotional needs be met in their important relationships with the significant others in their lives.

Restricted by rigid cultural expectations, however, many men still struggle with the notion of allowing themselves to simply be aware of their own emotions and their feelings. As author Liz Plank points out in her book, *For the Love of Men, A New Vision for Mindful Masculinity*, our idealized and culturally-based notions of masculinity not only encourage men to repress their emotions, it creates shame for them about feeling these feelings in the first place.[6] Plank describes the expectation of our society which teaches men that they don't have emotional needs, and that they should feel embarrassed when these needs naturally occur. She hypothesizes that some men and boys may express aggressive behavior because they lack the social permission to express their emotions in the first place. Plank describes the pact of idealized masculinity as a vicious cycle. It makes men feel shame and then enforces the rule that makes shame impossible to talk about.[7] As a consequence, several of the women that Plank communicated with about their relationships with the men in their lives complained that their husbands and male partners appeared to them to be emotionally stunted and, consequently, were unable to participate in emotionally healthy relationships with them.[8] Some men also struggle with the issue of acknowledging intense negative feelings. The armed forces, for instance, is finally beginning to reckon with the problem of the unusually high suicide rate of veterans, who are expected to live up to the role of the stoic American male, where real men are not encouraged to acknowledge their deepest feelings of fear, grief and anger. In responding to this issue, beginning in January, 2023, all U. S. military veterans experiencing a suicide crisis will be eligible for free care at any VA or private facility, as the armed forces is now beginning to acknowledge the gravity of this problem.[9]

Bill Hawley, a Prevention Specialist employed by the Public Health Department of Johnson County, Wyoming, attempts to reconnect men to their feelings in a state where too often "real men" are supposed to be stoic and tough. Wyoming currently has the highest suicide rate in the country, the majority of whom are adult white males. Bill attempts to connect with vulnerable, isolated men, many of whom are disabled veterans. Having struggled in the past on a personal level with many of these issues himself, he strives to create a trusting, warm relationship with each of his clients as he travels throughout the county, visiting with them in their homes. By encouraging these men to speak about their unresolved feelings and problems, he helps them to connect with their inner feelings of hopelessness, rage, and anger. Bill hopes to aid in the creation of a new kind of American masculinity, one where "real Men" are allowed to experience their inner emotions and feelings as human beings.[10]

It's important to remember that the current degree of social awareness and interest regarding creating partnership that we enjoy today could not have been possible without the significant changes that occurred during the latter half of the twentieth and into the twenty-first century. Significant economic and cultural changes took place which up-ended the status-quo between the sexes. The importance of a minimum educational requirement of a high school degree for most employment, along with the possibility of higher education for some, helped to create new possibilities for everyone. The 1960's civil rights movement, the "feminist" revolution of the 1970's, the significant loss of good-paying male blue-collar manufacturing jobs in the 1980's, combined with women's entrance into the job market in large numbers in that same decade, have all contributed to these cultural upheavals. These persistent and expansive movements gave many the expectation that for the first time in our history true equality, along with freedom of expression, could be a right held by everyone.

When I look at old photographs of my paternal grandparents, married circa 1910, I remind myself that the culturally based codependent behaviors that many of us struggle to free ourselves from today were considered "normal" in my grandparents' time. A wife in that time period would have been expected to be compliant and not overly assertive or argumentative with her husband, as her relationship with him was not based on equality. She would not have been expected to follow her own personal goals or ambitions, nor to voice her own opinions too frequently. At that time, a man would have been expected to have the last word in all important decision-making in the household, often even those concerning child-rearing. A man would have expected obedience from his wife in all important area of decision-making, and he would have expected neither arguments nor opposing viewpoints from her.

Liz Plank addresses some of the changes we now need to make in changing our expectations for both genders. She asserts that the expectations that create limitations for both men and women in terms of their gender roles are born out of the same system and the same ideology. In order to accurately view these limitations, we must stop thinking whether one or the other is the victim or perpetrator, the winner or the loser. Plank states that men can approach their gender consciously as women have been learning to do, by practicing "mindful masculinity." She continues: "Freeing ourselves of gender rules doesn't mean that we have to remove it entirely from our lives, but rather that we can take and leave the parts that make sense; we are all afforded the personal freedom to make those decisions personally and privately." Plank concludes by saying, "This isn't an attack on personal freedom; it's an extension of it."[11]

Plank concludes that, ultimately, in today's world, the problem is not that women are trying to make men "more feminine;" the problem is that the world itself and its expectations are becoming more feminine. Put another way, the skills and characteristics that we traditionally associate with women are now becoming more valuable in our world. Because of this change, it is important that we also change the way we raise boys.[12] Mindful masculinity could help men cultivate skills such as emotional intelligence, become more aware and conscious of their internal dialogues, become more aware of the intentions behind their actions and become more aware of the reason why they do what they do. According to Plank, for men, mindful masculinity is essentially about taking back control of themselves.[13]

Creating Partnerships

Taking part in a successful partnership can be a liberating personal experience. Creating a partnership can also be challenging; not always loving and peaceful, the ride can be bumpy, the progress uneven. And yet, occasional messiness experienced in relationships can be a valuable way to increase our own self-awareness. As we learn about the other people in our lives, we can also learn about ourselves and how we react to conflict. Learning to resolve conflicts can also help us build skills that are essential for committed relationships, such as listening, communicating and tolerating differences.

My own experience with conflict shows a similar development. Prior to embracing a partnership ethic, I would approach interactions with those I cared about with a combination of tentativeness and insecurity. I often avoided conflict by waiting for others to take charge, make suggestions and take responsibility. Although not perfect, today my efforts in this area are significantly more proactive and are based on a growing confidence in my ability to communicate clearly, tolerate potential conflict and take responsibility for decision-making with those I care about.

So, what, then, is it like to engage in a successful partnership? For some, this type of relationship may seem unremarkable, as a comfortable, normal process, especially for experienced, committed partners. When I've spent time with older, happily married couples, for instance, I sense that they routinely operate as partners, no matter how their relationship may have begun, often decades earlier. They appear to work together seamlessly, often without even speaking. For many, couples like these can be models for what healthy relationships can look like.

Although many of us agree that the objective of partnership is important and valuable, the goal often seems elusive. One reason could be that many of us don't have enough experience in engaging in cooperative relationships based on equality. Many may feel that successful partnerships happen either by accident, or just evolve naturally. We may feel happy when one of our relationships evolves into workable teamwork, but how many of us stop to consider how this process occurs? Although many agree that partnerships are the optimal type of relationship, they may not know how to consciously create them. I sometimes feel that in creating partnerships many of us may just be making it all up as we go along.

The following are some guidelines agreed upon myself and others who have been working for some time towards creating partnerships with those we care about. They are meant as general suggestions only, and should apply to any two individuals who wish to engage in a partnership, regardless of their gender or the type of relationship they are engaged in.

For me the cornerstone of partnership is expressing the intention to create a partnership with another person. Communicating this intention is key. A basic sense of equality should pervade the relationship, even while each partner has their particular areas of expertise. If a husband has experience in car maintenance, for instance, partners could agree that he should take charge in that area. Similarly, if a wife routinely files the tax returns, then she could claim control in that area. In other areas of their lives, however, couples' decision-making could be more or less fluid, after considerable communication, collaboration and negotiation.

Both members need to be committed to engage in partnership and to participate with each other as equals. Those raised as non-dominants may need to learn to be more proactive and assertive in communicating their needs. Those raised as dominants may need to learn to relinquish control of the actions of their partner and practice skills in listening, negotiating and cooperating. Both members will need to learn to deal with the uncertainty of loss of control over the other as each attempts to navigate with each other in this uncertain terrain. At times partners may feel confused, anxious or uncertain as to what to say or how to say it. If situations such as these arise, it's important to feel safe in the process of communicating and listening to each other, as each member will most likely experience new feelings regarding their changing relationship.

Creating a working relationship is difficult; yet, I believe partners have to maintain their commitment to continue with the work, until both feel comfortable with what they've achieved. Engaging in a partnership is a conscious commitment, not only to your partner, but also to yourself; it's a process that entails hard work, trust, patience, humility and mutual respect.

This process is not easy. We will all make mistakes. Codependent patterns will emerge. Non-dominants may resort to "people pleasing" or in acquiescing too easily to create a safe outcome in a discussion. Dominant individuals may find themselves raising their voices or issuing orders. This is part of the learning process. Mistakes will be inevitable. If we fall short, it's okay to mess up. If we fail, we can always stop and start the process all over again.

Partners should learn to give up the "It's either you or me" attitude that often arises when disagreements occur. There are a variety of solutions for this dilemma. A few possibilities are: 1. Agree to disagree and end the discussion (at least for the short-term); 2. Negotiate to find a compromise solution both parties can agree to; 3. Agree that one party's solution is the correct one; 4. Agree that more information is needed to find a solution that both can agree to.

Other issues to keep in mind may be the following: 1) Partnership will not look the same for everyone. Partners must decide for themselves what a healthy relationship looks like for them. 2) Partners must learn to trust each other as well as to be trustworthy; commitments must be honored on both sides, whenever possible. 3) Each person should learn to express his or her own thoughts and ideas clearly, directly and independently. 4) Each member must maintain and express respect for the other's beliefs, even if they're different from their own. 5) Whenever possible, partners must learn to listen to each other without interruptions. 6) Partners need to learn to ask for help when they need to instead of trying to do everything themselves. A woman, for instance, could ask for help cleaning up the kitchen after a meal, or a man could ask for help for a second pair of hands for carpentry or plumbing. 7) When necessary, individuals will need to set limits against what could be considered unacceptable behaviors by their partners. If a "red line" has been crossed, this should be communicated and limits set firmly. 8) Partners must be prepared to occasionally step outside of their comfort zones and take verbal risks; they should also understand the possibility of "surprise" outcomes from these interactions. 9) Finally, members of a pair should often acknowledge and express gratitude for the efforts of their partner, especially in an area where they may not have a great deal of understanding or experience themselves.

While creating their relationship, partners should each feel they are able to develop, express and honor themselves, as well as their partners, as unique individuals. Partners should be aware that the relationship that they're creating is organic, a work in progress which will continually change and grow. An equal relationship should make partners feel comfortable, safe and secure with each other. Lastly, those taking part in a successful partnership should know that what they have achieved is extremely valuable and definitely worth all of their efforts and hard work, a happy, successful event to be celebrated.

I'd like to leave you with this thought. Although none of us can assume that by engaging in caring, respectful partnerships, based on equality, mutual respect and trust we can solve all of our society's serious and pressing problems, it is one place where we can all begin.

Notes

Introduction

1. Rachel Simmons, *The Curse of the Good Girl* (New York: The Penguin Press, 2010), 10.
2. John Lee, *The Flying Boy* (Deerfield Beach, FL: Health Communications , Inc., 1987), 27.

Chapter 1

1. Robert Subby, *Lost in the Shuffle: The Codependent Reality* (Deerfield Beach, FL: Health Communications, Inc., 1987), 15.
2. Adult Children of Alcoholics World Service Organization, *Adult Children of Alcoholic/Dysfunctional Families*, (Torrance, CA: Adult Children of Alcoholics World Service Organization, 2006) 100.
3. Melody Beatty, *Codependent No More*, (New York: A Hazelden Book/Harper Collins Publishers, 1987) 37.
4. Beatty, *Codependent No More*, 17.
5. Mellody, Miller and Miller, *Facing Codependence*, 7.
6. Mellody, Miller and Miller, *Facing Codependence*, 8.
7. Adult Children of Alcoholics World Service Organization, *Adult Children of Alcoholics*, 101.
8. Beatty, *Codependent No More*, 15.

9. Duke Robinson, *Too Nice For Your Own Good* (Warner Books, 1997), xvi.

10. Robinson, *Too Nice For Your Own Good*, xvii.

11. Robinson, *Too Nice For Your Own Good*, 23.

12. Sharon Wegscheider Cruse, *Another Chance—Hope and Health for the Alcoholic* (Science and Behavior Books, Palo Alto, CA, 1989), 249.

13. Subby, *Lost in the Shuffle*, 22.

14. Stephanie Abbott, Melody Beattie, Brian DesRoches, Marshall Hardy , John Hough, Roseann Lloyd, Veronica Ray, Brenda Schaeffer, Jennifer Schneider, *Talk, Trust and Feel: Keeping Codependency Out Of Your Life,* (New York: A Hazelden book/Ballantine Book, 1991), 48.

15. Abbot, et al, *Talk, Trust and Feel*, 49.

16. Abbot, et al, *Talk, Trust and Feel*, 51.

17. 18. Barry K. Weinhold and Janae B. Weinhold, *Breaking Free of the Codependent Trap*, (New York: MJF Books, 1989), 87.

18. Weinhold, and Weinhold, *Breaking Free of the Codependent Trap*, 88.

19. Weinhold and Weinhold, *Breaking Free of the Codependent Trap*, 89.

20. Beatty, *Codependent No More*, 70.

21. Charles L. Whitfield, *Healing the Child Within*, (Deerfield Beach, FL: Health Communications, 1989), 69.

22. Beatty, *Codependent No More*, 84.

23. Beatty, *Codependent No More*, 83.

24. Robert J. Ackerman, *Perfect Daughters: Adult Daughters of Alcoholics,* (Deerfield Beach, FL: Health Communications, Inc.) 119.

25. Ackerman, *Perfect Daughters*, 33.

26. Ackerman, *Perfect Daughters*, 35.

27. Mellody, Miller and Miller, *Facing Codependence*, xxii.

28. Thomas Szasz, *The Myth of Mental Illness,* (New York: Harper Collins Publishers, 1974), 262.

29. Subby, *Lost in the Shuffle*, 10.

30. Mellody, Miller and Miller, *Facing Codependence*, xxii.

31. CoDA Service Office, *Co-Dependents Anonymous*, (Phoenix, AZ: CoDA Service Office, 1995), iii.

32. Weinhold and Weinhold, *Breaking Free of the Codependent Trap*, 28.

33. Marshall Hardy and John Hough, *Against the Wall, Men's Reality in a Codependent Culture (*New York: Hazelden Book/Ballantine Book, 1991), 48.

34. Hardy and Hough, *Against the Wall,* 50.

Chapter 2

1. Robert Subby, *Lost in the Shuffle: The Codependent Reality* (Deerfield Beach, FL: Health Communications, Inc., 1987), 17.

2. Melody Beatty, *Codependent No More* (New York: A Hazelden Book/Harper Collins Publishers, 1987), 22.

3. Carol Gilligan, "Mommy, I Know You," *Newsweek*, January 30, 2006.

4. **CoDA Service Office, *Co-Dependents Anonymous* (Phoenix, AZ: CoDA Service Office, 1995**), v.

5. Allan G. Johnson, *The Gender Knot: Unraveling Our Patriarchal Legacy* (Philadelphia, PA: Temple University Press, 1997), 252.

6. Johnson, *The Gender Knot*, 252.

7. Barry K. Weinhold and Janae B. Weinhold, *Breaking Free of the Codependent Trap* (New York: MJF Books, 1989), 29.
8. Riane Eisler, *The Power of Partnership* (Novato, CA: New World Library, 2002),15.
9. Johnson, *The Gender Knot*, 253.

Chapter 3

1. Riane Eisler, *The Chalice and the Blade, Our History, Our Future* (New York: Harper Collins Publishers, 1988),244; Note: This chronology by Andre Leroi-Gourhan, director of the Sorbonne's Center for Pre-historic and Protohistoric Studies dates the chronology of the Paleolithic cave art from approximately 30,000 B.C.E to 10,000 B.C.E.
2. Eisler, *The Chalice and the Blade*, 6.
3. Merlin Stone, *When God was a Woman*, (New York: Harcourt Brace & Company, 1976),13.
4. Gerda Lerner, *The Creation of Patriarchy,* (Oxford University Press, 1986), 148.
5. Marilyn French, *Beyond Power,* (New York: Random House 1985), 44.
6. Eisler, *The Chalice and the Blade*, 7.
7. Marija Gimbutas, *Gods and Goddess of Old Europe* (Berkeley and Los Angeles, CA: University of California Press,1996),152.
8. Stone, *When God was a Woman*, 23.
9. Stone, *When God was a Woman*, 19.
10. Barbara Mor and Monica Sjoo, *The Great Cosmic Mother: Rediscovering the Religion of the Earth* (San Francisco, CA: Harper and Row, Publishers, 1987), 89.
11. Eisler, *The Chalice and the Blade,* 14.

12. Eisler, *The Chalice and the Blade*, 14.

13. Eisler, *The Chalice and the Blade*, 28. Note: On page p. 27 in *The Chalice and the Blade*, Eisler points out that in our culture, which is built on the ideas of hierarchy and ranking and in-group versus out-group thinking, rigid differences and polarities are emphasized. She points out that ours is a dichotomized, either/or thinking that philosophers from earliest times have cautioned can lead to a simplistic misreading of reality.

14. Mor and Sjoo, *The Great Cosmic Mother*, 213.

15. Jeanne Achterberg, *Woman as Healer* (Boston, MA: Shambhala Publications, 1990) 15.

16. Achterberg, *Woman as Healer*, 27.

17. Achterberg, *Woman as Healer*, 30.

18. Eisler, *The Chalice and the Blade,* 43.

19. Gimbutas, *Gods and Goddesses of Old Europe*, 18.

20. Eisler, *The Chalice and the Blade,* 44.

21. Gimbutas, *Gods and Goddesses of Old Europe*, 18.

22. French, *Beyond Power*, 48.

23. Eisler, *The Chalice and the Blade*, 48.

24. French, *Beyond Power,* 87.

25. Stone, *When God was a Woman*, 176. Note: Eisler points out in *The Chalice and the Blade,* p. 93, that this fact is remarkable in light of the archaeological evidence showing that long after the Hebrew invasions the people of Canaan, including the Hebrews themselves, continued to worship a female goddess.

26. Stone, *When God Was a Woman.* 176. Note: Eisler points out in *The Chalice and the Blade,* page 93, that this fact is remarkable in light of the archaeological evidence showing that long after the Hebrew invasions the

people of Canaan, including the Hebrews themselves, continued to worship a female goddess

27. Bart Ehrman, *Misquoting Jesus* (San Francisco, CA: Harper Collins Publishers, 2005) 179.

28. Achterberg, *Woman as Healer*, 67.

29. Achterberg, *Woman as Healer*, 42.

30. Barbara Ehrenreich and Dierdre English, *Witches, Midwives and Nurses*, (Old Westbury, NY: The Feminist Press, SUNY, 1973) 6.

31. Ehrenreich and English, *Witches, Midwives and Nurses*, 15.

32. Achterberg, *Woman as Healer*, 79.

33. Achterberg, *Woman as Healer*, 81.

34. Ehrenreich and English, *Witches, Midwives and Nurses*, 13.

35. Ehrenreich and English, *Witches, Midwives and Nurses*, 85.

36. Elizabeth Gilbert, *Committed* (New York: Viking Penguin, a member of the Penguin Group, 2010) 65.

37. Gilbert, *Committed*, 66.

38. Barbara Ehrenreich and Dierdre English, *For Her Own Good* (New York: Anchor Books, a division of Random House, Inc., Second Edition, 2005) 9.

39. Carol Tavris, *The Mismeasure of Woman* (New York: Touchstone: Simon and Schuster, 1992) 264.

40. Stephanie Cootnz, *Marriage, a History*, (New York: Viking Penguin Group, 2005) 125.

41. Eisler, *Sacred Pleasure*, (San Francisco, CA: Harper Collins, 1995) 109.

42. Michael Kimmel, *Manhood in America*, (The Free Press: A Division of Simon and Schuster, Inc., 1996) 20.

43. Kimmel, *Manhood in America*, 23.

44. Kimmel, *Manhood in America*, 26.

45. Tavris, *The Mismeasure of Woman*, 265.

46. Robert L.Griswold, *Fatherhood in America*, (New York: Harper Collins Publishers, Inc., 1993) 14.

47. Griswold, *Fatherhood in America*, 142.

48. Ann Crittenden, *The Price of Motherhood*, (New York: Henry Holt and Company, LLC., 2001) 47.

49. Ehrenreich and English. *For Her Own Good,* 116.

50. Anna Fels, *Necessary Dreams*, (New York: Random House, 2004) 170.

51. Kate Millett, *Sexual Politics* (New York: Avon Books, 1971) 108.

52. Virginia Wolf, *A Room of One's Own* (New York: Harcourt Brace and Co., Inc., 1929) 123.

53. Fels, *Necessary Dreams*, 170.

54. Fels, *Necessary Dreams*, 174.

55. French, *Beyond Power*, 212.

56. French, *Beyond Power*, 213.

57. Betty Friedan, *The Feminine Mystique,* (New York: W. W. Norton and Company, 2001) 16.

58. Freidan, *The Feminine Mystique*, 22.

59. Freidan, *The Feminine Mystique*, 24.

60. Fels, *Necessary Dreams,* 179.

61. Fels, *Necessary Dreams*, 180.

62. Faludi, *Stiffed: The Betrayal of the American Man,* (New York: William Morrow and Company, Inc., 1999) 51.

63. Faludi, *Stiffed,* 38.

64. Kimmel, *Manhood in America,* 265.

65. Barbara Ehrenreich, *The Hearts of Men*, (Garden City, NY: Anchor Press/Doubleday, 1984) 116.

66. Ehrenreich, *The Hearts of Men*, 12.

67. Kimmel, *Manhood in America*, 281.

68. Griswold, *Fatherhood in America*, 247.
69. Griswold, *Fatherhood in America*, 248.
70. Griswold, *Fatherhood in America*, 252.
71. Tony Dokoupil,"Why I Am Leaving Guyland," *Newsweek*, September 8, 2008.
72. Jane Riblett Wilkie, "The Decline in Men's Labor Force Participation and Income and the Changing Structure of Family Economic Support," *Journal of Marriage and the Family* 53, February 1991, 111-122.
73. Rachel Homer, and Karen Kornbluh, , "Paycheck Feminism," *MS.*, Fall, 2009.
74. Griswold, *Fatherhood in America*, 222.
75. Wilkie"The Decline in Men's Labor Force Participation and Income and the Changing Structure of Family Economic Support, *Journal of Marriage and the Family*, 53.
76. Barbara Kantrowitz and Pat Wingert, "Unmarried with Children," *Newsweek*, May 28, 2001.
77. Riane Eisler, *Dissolution: No Fault Divorce, Marriage and the Future of Women,* (New York: toExcel Publishing, 1998) 44.
78. Crittenden, *The Price of Motherhood*, 6.
79. Eisler, *Dissolution*, 107.
80. Nadia Mustafa, Ulla Plon and Dierdre van Dyke,"Who says a woman can't be Einstein?," *Time,* March 7, 2005.
81. Marie McCullough, "Surgeon Takes on a Whole New Operation," Philadelphia *Inquirer,* August 12, 2007.
82. Selma Moidel Smith, "Honors to Her Honor," *Experience*, 15:1, Fall 2004.
83. Tim McGirk,"Crossing the Line," *Time,* February 27, 2006.

84. Anna Quindlen, "Not Semi-Soldiers," *Newsweek* , November 12, 2007.

85. Kimmel, *Manhood in America*, 333.

Chapter 4

1.   Allan G. Johnson, *The Gender Knot, Unraveling Our Patriarchal Legacy* (Philadelphia, PA: Temple University Press, 1997) 61.

2.   Johnson, *The Gender Knot*, 62.

3.   Carol Tavris, *The Mismeasure of Woman,* (New York: Touchstone: Simon and Schuster, 1992) 92. Note: On page 91 Tavris points out that studies of aggression have often based on the assumption that men are aggressive and that females, in not behaving like males, are the opposite, or non-aggressive or submissive. She adds that most studies do not show that women are submissive or non-aggressive; rather, that women are, under certain conditions, less likely than men to behave aggressively. She summarizes by stating that in labeling women's behavior as the opposite of men's we not only are mistaken, we also lose critical information about women's ability to be aggressive.

4.   Johnson, *The Gender Knot*, 8. Note: On page 8 Johnson elaborates that our society is male centered in that our focus and attention is primarily about men and what they do. He adds that our society is male identified in that we value masculine qualities and values (as opposed to feminine) in most areas of endeavor such as business, politics, law, medicine and academia. Lastly, Johnson points out that our society is male dominated in that men dominate the major institutions of our

society; for the most part, women play peripheral roles, especially in the higher echelons of these institutions.

5. John Bradshaw, *Creating Love: The Next Stage of Growth,* (New York: Bantam Books, 1992) 27.

6. Bradshaw, *Creating, Love, The Next Stage of Growth*, 27.

7. Germaine Greer, *The Whole Woman* (New York: Random House, Inc, 1999) 133.

8. Bradshaw, *Creating Love, The Next Stage of Growth*, 26.

9. Johnson, *The Gender Knot*, 18.

10. Johnson, *The Gender Knot*, 218.

11. Johnson, *The Gender Knot*, 98.

12. Tavris, *The Mismeasure of Woman,* 302.

13. John Gray, *Men Are From Mars, Women Are From Venus*, (New York: Harper Collins Publishers, 1992) 16.

14. Gray, *Men Are From Mars, Women Are From Venus*, 18.

15. Anna Fels, *Necessary Dreams,* (New York: Random House, 2004) 16.

16. Fels, *Necessary Dreams*, 24.

17. Marie C. Wilson, *Closing the Leadership Gap: Why Women Can and Must Help Run the World,* (London: Penguin Books, Ltd., 2004) 54.

18. Fels, *Necessary Dreams*, 48.

19. Fels, *Necessary Dreams*, 50.

20. Fels*, Necessary Dreams*, 51.

21. Mary Pipher, *Reviving Ophelia: Saving the Selves of Adolescent Girls* (New York: The Penguin Group 1994) 39.

22. Jean Baker Miller, *Toward a New Psychology of Women* (Boston, MA, Beacon Press, 1986) 50.

23. R. William Betcher and William S. Pollack*, In a Time of Fallen Heroes: The Recreation of Masculinity*, (New York: The Guilford Press, 1993) 45.

24. Gray, *Men Are From Mars,* 18.
25. Gray, *Men Are From Mars*, 19.
26. Gray, *Men are From Mars*, 148.
27. Gray, *Men are From Mars*, 144.
28. Harriett Goldhor Lerner, *The Dance of Anger: A Woman's Guide to Changing the Patterns of Intimate Relationships* (New York: Harper and Collins, Publishers, 1985) 50.
29. Johnson, *The Gender Knot*, 27.
30. Michael Kimmel, *Guyland: The Perilous World Where Boys Become Men* (New York: Harper Collins Publishers, 2008) 47. Note: On this page Kimmel quotes the playwright David Mamet, who says, "Women have, in men's minds, such a low place on the social ladder of this country that it's useless to define yourself in terms of a women. What men need is men's approval."
31. Gloria Steinem, *Revolution from Within* (Boston, MA: Little, Brown and Company, 1992) 257.
32. Steinem, *Revolution from Within*, 257.
33. Tavris, *The Mismeasure of Woman*, 63. Note: Tavris adds that in spite of this fact, the obligation of fulfilling these responsibilities today usually falls to women.
34. Tavris, *The Mismeasure of Woman*, 64.
35. Tavris, *The Mismeasure of Woman*, 67
36. Beryl Lieff Benderly, *The Myth of Two Minds: What Gender Means and Doesn't Mean* (New York: Doubleday Publishing, 1987) 214.
37. Nadia Mustafa, Ulla Plon and Dierdre van Dyk, "Who Says a Woman Can't Be Einstein?" *Time.* March 7, 2005.
38. Mustafa, Plon and van Dyk, "Who Says a Woman Can't Be Einstein?" *Time.*

39. Sharon Begley, "Math is Hard, Barbie Said," *Newsweek*, October 27, 2008.

40. Mustafa, Plon and van Dyk, "Who Says a Woman Can't Be Einstein?" *Time*.

41. Sharon Begley, "Pink Brain, Blue Brain," *Newsweek*, September 14, 2009.

42. Dan Kindlon and Michael Thompson, *Raising Cain: Protecting the Emotional Life of Boys,* (New York: Random House Publishing Group, 2000) 13.

43. Kindlon and Thompson, *Raising Cain,* 14.

44. Marshall Hardy and John Hough, *Against the Wall,* (New York: A Hazelden Book: Ballantine Books, 1991) 1.

45. Hardy and Hough, *Against the Wall,* 161.

46. Kay Hagan, "Codependency and the Myth of Recovery, a Feminist Scrutiny," in Marguerite Babcock and Christine McKay, Eds., *Challenging Codependency: Feminist Critiques,* (Toronto, CA: University of Toronto Press, 1995) 203.

47. Hardy and Hough, *Against the Wall,* 7.

48. Hardy and Hough, *Against the Wall,* 163.

49. Hardy and Hough, *Against the Wall,* 164.

50. John Bradshaw, *Healing the Shame That Binds You,* (Deerfield Beach, FL: Health Communications, Inc. 1988) 14.

Chapter 5

1. Mary Pipher, *Reviving Ophelia: Saving the Selves of Adolescent Girls* (New York: The Penguin Group, 1994) 18.

2. Carol Gilligan, *In a Different Voice* (Cambridge, MA: Harvard University Press, 1982) 12.

3. Gilligan, *In A Different Voice*, 13.
4. Pipher, *Reviving Ophelia*, 20.
5. Pipher, *Reviving Ophelia*, 22.
6. Rachel Simmons, *The Curse of the Good Girl* (New York: The Penguin Press, 2010) 3.
7. Simmons, *The Curse of the Good Girl*, 6.
8. Simmons, *The Curse of the Good Girl*, 9.
9. Simmons, *The Curse of the Good Girl*, 10.
10. Germaine Greer, *The Whole Woman* (New York: Random House, Inc., 1999) 222.
11. Elizabeth Gilbert, *Committed* (New York: Viking Penguin, a member of the Penguin Group (USA) Inc.) 163.
12. Janice P. Haaken, "A Critical Analysis of the Codependency Construct" in Babcock and McKay, Eds., *Challenging Codependency* (Toronto, CN: University of Toronto Press, 1995) 55.
13. Haaken, "A Critical Analysis of the Codependency Construct" in *Challenging Codependency*, 59.
14. Maryanne Walters, "The Codependent Cinderella Who Loves Too Much. . . Fights Back." In Babcock and McKay, Eds., *Challenging Codependency* (Toronto, CN: University of Toronto Press, 1995) 184.
15. Anna Fels, *Necessary Dreams (New York: Random House, 2004) 54.*
16. Gilligan, *In A Different Voice, 17.*
17. Jean Baker Miller, *Toward a New Psychology of Women,* (Boston, MA: Beacon Press, 1986) *62.*
18. Miller,*Toward a New Psychology of Women, 19.*
19. Miller,*Toward a New Psychology of Women, 19.*
20. Gilligan, *In A Different Voice, 67.*
21. Gilligan, *In A Different Voice, 67.*

22. Kevin Leman, *The Pleasers: Women Who Can't Say No--And The Men Who Control them* (The Bantam Doubleday Dell Publishing Group 1987) 26.

23. Crittenden, Ann, *The Price of Motherhood* (New York: Henry Holt and Co., LLC, 2001), 2.

24. Crittenden, *The Price of Motherhood*, 8.

25. Crittenden, *The Price of Motherhood*, 6.

26. Hamilton, "The Money Queens," *Time,* April 16, 2007.

27. Kantrowitz, "Women and Leadership/Women and Power," *Newsweek*, October 15, 2007.

28. Paula Johnson, "Women and Power: Toward a Theory of Effectiveness," *Journal of Social Issues*, Vol. 32, No. 3.

29. Johnson, "Women and Power: Toward a Theory of Effectiveness," *Journal of Social Issues*, 103.

30. "WorkplaceAnger—WhoWins?"in http://www.cnn.com/2007/LIVING/worklife/08/02/angry.men.women.reut/index.html.

31. Carol S. Dweck, Therese E. Goetz and Nan L. Strauss, "Sex Differences in Learned Helplessness: IV. An Experimental and Naturalistic Study of Failure Generalization and its Mediators," *Journal of Personality and Social Psychology.* 1980, Vol. 38, No. 3.

32. Gloria Steinem, *Revolution from Within*, (Boston, MA: Little, Brown and Company, 1992) 120.

33. Steinem, *Revolution from Within*, 120.

34. Nancy Gibbs, "College Confidential," *Time,* April 14, 2008.

35. Anna Quindlen, "The Leadership Lid," *Newsweek,* October 13, 2008.

36. American Association of University Women, "For Women, Equal Pay? No Way," *Time*, May 7, 2007.

37. Sarah Ball, Jessica Bennett, Jesse Ellison,"Are We There Yet?," *Newsweek,* March 29, 2010.

38. Irene H. Frieze, Josephine E. Olson, Audry J. Murrell and Mano S. Selvan, "Work Values and Their Effect on Work Behavior and Work Outcomes in Female and Male Managers," *Sex Roles*, Vol. 54, No. 1 – 2, January 2006.

39. Kathleen McCartney, Deborah Phillips and Sandra Scarr, "Working Mothers and Their Families," *American Psychologist*, Vol. 44, No. 11, November 1989.

40. Arlie Russell Hochschild, *The Second Shift,* (New York: Penguin Books) 148.

41. Hochschild, *The Second Shift*, 29.

42. Rosalind Barnett and Caryl Rivers, *She Works, He Works,* (Cambridge, MA: Harvard University Press) 27.

43. Hochschild, *The Second Shift,* 4.

44. Hochschild, *The Second Shift*, 8.

45. Lois Wladis Hoffman "Effects of Maternal Employment in the Two-Parent Family," *American Psychologist*, Vol. 44, No. 2, February 1989.

46. Barnett and Rivers, *She Works, He Works*, 36.

47. Barnett and Rivers, *She Works, He Works*, 37.

48. Carol Tavris, *The Mismeasure of Woman*, (New York: Touchstone: Simon and Schuster, 1992) 203.

49. Gloria Feldt, *No Excuses*, (Berkeley, CA: Seal Press, 2010) 82.

50. Feldt, *No Excuses*, 82.

Chapter 6

1. William July II, *Understanding the Tin Man: Why So Many Men Avoid Intimacy* (New York: Broadway Books) 76.

2. July, *Understanding the Tin Man*, 75.
3. Dan Kindlon and Michael Thompson, *Raising Cain*: *Protecting the Emotional Life of Boys*, (New York: Random House, 2000) 15.
4. Kindlon and Thompson, *Raising Cain*, 13.
5. Kindlon and Thompson, *Raising Cain*, 16.
6. William Pollack, *Real Boys*, (New York: Henry Holt and Company, 1998) 23.
7. Pollack, *Real Boys*, 24.
8. William R. Betcher and William S. Pollack, *In a Time of Fallen Heroes: The Re-creation of Masculinity* (New York: The Guilford Press, 1993) 41.
9. Pollack, *Real Boys*, 146.
10. Pollack, *Real Boys,* 148.
11. Kindlon and Thompson, *Raising Cain*, 74.
12. Kindlon and Thompson, *Raising Cain*, 75.
13. Niobe Way, "Using Feminist Research Methods to Understand the Friendships of Adolescent Boys," *Journal of Social Issues*, Vol. 53, No. 4, 1997.
14. Betcher and Pollack, *In a Time of Fallen Heroes*, 38.
15. Betcher and Pollack, *In a Time of Fallen Heroes*, 40.
16. Kindlon and Thompson, *Raising Cain*, 43.
17. Peg Tyre,"The Trouble With Boys," *Newsweek,* January 30, 2006.
18. Peg Tyre,"The Trouble With Boys," *Newsweek,* January 30, 2006.
19. Lev Grossman, "The Secret Love Lives of Teenage Boys," *Time*, September 4, 2006.
20. Michael Kimmel, *Guyland: The Perilous World Where Boys Become Men,* (New York: Harper Collins Publishers, 2008), 25.
21. Kimmel, *Guyland*, 28.

22. Kimmel, *Guyland*, 34.
23. Kimmel, *Guyland*, 48.
24. Joseph H. Pleck, *The Myth of Masculinity* (Cambridge, MA: MIT Press, 1987) 24.
25. Pleck, *The Myth of Masculinity*, 23.
26. Kimmel, *Guyland*, 63. Note: on p. 281 Kimmel argues that the only way to transform the culture of Guyland is to break the culture of silence that sustains it. Young men involve themselves in excessive, sexist, violent and anti-social behaviors in part because they believe the other guys won't confront them and that the community will back them up. According to Kimmel, to end the culture of silence, bystanders must learn to be whistleblowers, and to behave independently from perpetrators.
27. Kimmel, *Guyland*, 227.
28. Allan G. Johnson, *The Gender Knot: Unraveling Our Patriarchal Legacy* (Philadelphia, PA: Temple University Press, 1997) 111.
29. Marshall Hardy and John Hough, *Against the Wall: Men's Reality in a Codependent Culture*, New York: A Hazelden Book: Ballantine Books, 1991) 132.
30. Hardy and Hough, *Against the Wall*, 135.
31. Robert J. Ackerman, *Silent Sons: A Book For and About Men*, New York: Fireside Books, 1993) 41.
32. Hardy and Hough, 136.
33. Kimmel, *Guyland,* 85.
34. Johnson, *The Gender Knot*, 193.
35. Herb Goldberg, *The Hazards of Being Male: Surviving the Myth of Masculine Privilege* (Bergenfield, NJ: The New American Library, 1976), 58.
36. July, *The Tin Man*, 129.

37. July, *The Tin Man*, 129.
38. Hardy and Hough, *Against the Wall*, 137.
39. Kindlon and Thompson, *Raising Cain,* 104.
40. Kindlon and Thompson, *Raising Cain*, 106.
41. Robert Bly, *Iron John: A Book About Men,* (Reading, MA: Addison Wesley, 1990), 25.
42. Michael Schwalbe, *Unlocking the Iron Cage*, (New York: Oxford University Press, 1996) 78.
43. Bly, *Iron John,* 14.
44. Johnson, *The Gender Knot*, 194.
45. Johnson, *The Gender Knot*, 195.
46. Herb Goldberg, *The New Male: From Macho to Sensitive, But Still All Male* (Bergenfield, NJ: The New American Library,1979) 31.
47. Goldberg, *The New Male*, 32.
48. Goldberg, *The New Male*, 38.
49. Goldberg, *The Hazards of Being Male,* 59.
50. Johnson, *The Gender Knot*, 31.
51. Johnson, *The Gender Knot*, 28.
52. Johnson, *The Gender Knot*, 29.
53. Ackerman, *Silent Sons,* 51.
54. Goldberg, *The New Male,* 194.
55. Hardy and Hough, *Against the Wall*, 149.
56. Hardy and Hough, *Against the Wall*, 150.
57. Dan Mulhern, "How to be a Real Man," *Newsweek*, May 9, 2011.

Chapter 7

1. Jean Baker Miller, *Toward a New Psychology of Women* (Boston, MA: Beacon Press, 1986) 6.
2. Miller, *Toward a New Psychology of Women*, 7.
3. Miller, *Toward a New Psychology of Women*, 7.

4. Miller, Toward a New Psychology of Women, 8.

5. Miller, *Toward a New Psychology of Women*, 10.

6. Allan G. Johnson, *The Gender Knot: Unraveling Our Patriarchal Legacy* (Philadelphia, PA: Temple University Press, 1997) 20.

7. Anna Fels, *Necessary Dreams* (New York: Random House, 2004) 153.

8. Fels, *Necessary Dreams*, 154.

9. Goldberg, *The New Male-Female Relationship* (Bergenfield, NJ: The New American Library, 1984) 8.

10. Goldberg, *The New Male-Female Relationship*, 9.

11. Paula Johnson, "Women and Power: Toward a Theory of Effectiveness," *Journal of Social Issues*, Vol. 32, No. 3, 1976.

12. Kathleen Deveny, "We're Bossy—And Proud of it," *Newsweek*, June 30, 2008. Note: Kathleen Deveny further describes our ambivalence with female power by adding that, although telling other people what to do is thought of a leadership quality, it's a behavior that's tolerated more from men in authority, than from women.

13. William July II, *Understanding the Tin Man: Why So Many Men Avoid Intimacy* (New York: Broadway Books, 2001) 82.

14. Herb Goldberg, *The Hazards of Being Male* (Bergenfield, NJ: The New American Library, 1976) 12.

15. Johnson, *The Gender Knot*, 27

16. Elizabeth Janeway, *Man's World, Woman's Place* (New York: Dell Publishing Company, Inc., 1971) 48.

17. Warren Farrell, *Why Men Are The Way They Are* (New York: Berkeley Publishing Group, 1986) 10.

18. Herb Goldberg, *The New Male From Macho to Sensitive But Still All Male* (Bergenfield, NJ: The New American Library, 1979) 237.
19. Barry K. Weinhold and Janae B.Weinhold, *Breaking Free of the Codependent Trap* (New York: MJF Books, 1989) 52.
20. Goldberg, *The Hazards of Being Male,* 69.
21. Farrell, *Why Men Are The Way They Are,* xxii.
22. Harriett Goldhor Lerner, *The Dance of Anger: A Woman's Guide to Changing The Patterns of Intimate Relationships* (New York: Harper and Row, Publishers, 1985) 56.
23. Gloria Steinem, *Revolution From Within* (Boston, MA: Little, Brown and Company, 1992) *256.*
24. Steinem, *Revolution From Within,* 257.
25. Elizabeth Gilbert, *Committed* (New York: Viking Penguin a member of the Penguin Group (USA), 2010) 49.
26. M. Scott Peck, *The Road Less Traveled* (New York: Touchstone: Simon and Schuster, 1980) 89.
27. Peck, *The Road Less Traveled,* 90.
28. Peck, *The Road Less Traveled,* 92.
29. Peck, *The Road Less Traveled,* 92.
30. Robin Norwood, *Women Who Love Too Much* (New York: Simon and Schuster, 1997) 63.
31. Anne Wilson Schaef, *Women's Reality* (San Francisco, CA: Harper & Row, Publishers, 1985) 59.
32. Rosalind Barnett, Robert T.Brennan, Robin C. Gareis, "When She Earns More Than He Does: A Longitudinal Study of Dual-Earner Couples." *Journal of Marriage and Family* 63, February 2001.

33. Susan J. Douglas, *Enlightened Sexism*, (New York: Times Books, Henry Holt and Company, 2010) 3.

34. Douglas, *Enlightened Sexism*, 5.

35. Douglas, *Enlightened Sexism*, 299. Note: Douglas adds that, in addition, women are still expected to bear the major costs, in time and money, of caring for children and aging parents, as nearly 70 percent of unpaid caregivers of older adults are female. Douglas states further that the gap in poverty rates between men and women is wider in America than in anywhere else in the Western world.

36. Arlie Russel Hochschild, *The Second Shift* (New York: Penguin Books, 2003)266.

37. Goldberg, *The New Male-Female Relationship*, 20.

38. Steinem, *Revolution From Within*, 258.

39. Steinem, *Revolution From Within*, 259.

40. Vernon L. Quinsey, Robert C. Rowe, and William D. Walker, "Authoritarianism and Sexual Aggression," *Journal of Personal and Social Psychology*, 1993, Vol. 65, No. 5.

41. Kevin Leman, *The Pleasers: Women Who Can't Say No—And the Men Who Control Them* (New York: The Bantam Doubleday Dell Publishing Group, Inc.,, 1987) 171.

42. Patricia Evans, *The Verbally Abusive Relationship* (Avon, MA: Adams Media Corporation, 1996) 30.

43. Evans, *The Verbally Abusive Relationship*, 31.

44. Beverly Engel, *The Emotionally Abused Woman: Overcoming Destructive Patterns and Reclaiming Yourself*, (New York: Random House Publishing, 1990) 75.

45. Evans, *The Verbally Abusive Relationship*, 39.

46. Evans, *The Verbally Abusive Relationship*, 42.

47. "Misogyny: A Public Health Crisis," National Organization for Women, http://www.now.org/news/note/082207.html.

48. Judith Herman, *Trauma and Recovery,* (New York: Basic Books, 1992, 1997) 30.

49. Anna Quindlen "Not So Safe Back Home," *Newsweek,* April 7, 2003.

50. Jesse Ellison, "The Military's Secret Shame," *Newsweek,* April 11, 2011

51. Natalie Wilson,"Culture of Rape," *MS.,* Spring, 2010.

52. Jean Baker Miller, *Toward a New Psychology of Women,* (Boston, MA: Beacon Press, 1986) 17.

53. Elizabeth Janeway, *Man's World, Woman's Place,* (New York: Dell Publishing Company, 1971) 283.

54. Rosalind Barnett and Caryl Rivers, *She Works, He Works,* (Cambridge, MA: Harvard University Press, 1996) 215.

Chapter 8

1. *Co-Dependents Anonymous,* First Edition (Phoenix, AZ: CoDA Service Office, Phoenix, AZ, 1995) v.

2. Riane Eisler, *The Power of Partnership,* (Novato, CA: New World Library, 2002) 10.

3. John Bradshaw, *Healing the Shame that Binds You* (Deerfield Beach, FL: Health Communications, 1988) 163.

4. Jean Baker Miller, *Toward a New Psychology of Wome*n (Boston, MA: Beacon Press, 1986) 138.

5. M. Scott Peck, *The Road Less Traveled,* (New York: Touchstone: Simon and Schuster, 1980) 128

6. Bradshaw, *Creating Love: The Next Great Stage of Growth* (New York: Bantam Books, 1992) 44.

7. Peck, *The Road Less Traveled*, 168.
8. Patricia Evans, *The Verbally Abusive Relationship* (Avon, MA: Adams Media Corporation, 1996) 36.
9. Evans, *The Verbally Abusive Relationship*, 37.
10. Kahlil Gibran, *The Prophet*, (New York: Alfred A. Knopft, Publisher, 2009) 15.
11. Stephanie Coontz, *Marriage, a History*, (New York: Viking Penguin Group, 2005) 311.
12. Jessica Bennett and Jesse Ellison, "I don't. The Case Against Marriage," *Newsweek*, June 11, 2010.
13. Eisler, *The Power of Partnership,* xv.
14. Evans, *The Verbally Abusive Relationship*, 38.
15. Eisler, *The Power of Partnership*, 15.
16. Shel Silverstein, *The Missing Piece Meets the Big O* (New York: Harper & Row, Publishers, 1981).
17. Gloria Steinem, *Revolution From Within*, (Boston, MA: Little and Brown Company, 1992) 278.
18. R. William Betcher and William S. Pollack, *In a Time of Fallen Heroes—The Recreation of Masculinity* (New York: The Guilford Press, 1993) 15.
19. Herb Goldberg, *The New Male and Female Relationship* (Bergenfield, NJ: The New American Library, 1984) 175.
20. Goldberg, *The New Male and Female Relationship*, 176.
21. Goldberg, *The New Male and Female Relationship, 258.*
22. Allan G. Johnson, *The Gender Knot: Unraveling Our Patriarchal Legacy* (Philadelphia, PA: Temple University Press, 1997) 253.
23. Anne Wilson Schaef, *Women's Reality* (San Francisco, CA: Harper & Row, Publishers, 1985) 57.
24. Goldberg, *The New Male and Female Relationship, 172.*
25. Goldberg, *The New Male and Female Relationship*, 174.

26. Schaef, *Women's Reality*, 112.
27. Patricia O'Brien, "Why Men Don't Listen," *Working Women*, February, 1993.
28. O'Brien, "Why Men Don't Listen," *Working Woman*.
29. Daniel Goleman, *Emotional Intelligence* (New York: Bantam Books, 1997) 132.
30. Goleman, *Emotional Intelligence*, 143.
31. Judith Orloff, *Emotional Freedom* (New York: Three Rivers Press, 2009) 134.
32. Schaef, *Women's Reality*, 56.
33. Goldberg, *The New Male and Female Relationship*, 173.
34. Duke Robinson, *Too Nice For Your Own Good* (New York: Warner Books, 1997) 12.
35. Barry K.Weinhold and Janae B. Weinhold, *Breaking Free from the Codependent Trap* (New York: MJF Books, 1989) 211.
36. Robinson, *Too Nice For Your Own Good*, 17
37. Robinson, *Too Nice For Your Own Good*, 18.
38. Robinson, *Too Nice For Your Own Good*, 23.
39. Steinem, *Revolution From Within*, 279.
40. Johnson, *The Gender Knot*, 251.

Chapter 9

1. Gerda Lerner, *The Creation of Patriarchy,* (New York: Oxford University Press, 1986) 228.
2. Cynthia King, *Creating Partnerships: Unleashing Collaborative Power in the Workplace* (Santa Barbara: CA: Wisdom Way Press, 2005) 2.
3. King, *Creating Partnerships*, 3.
4. King, *Creating Partnerships*, 73.

5. Allan G. Johnson, *The Gender Knot: Unraveling Our Patriarchal Legacy* (Philadelphia, PA: Temple University Press, 1997) 249.

6. Riane Eisler, *Sacred Pleasure* (San Francisco, CA: Harper Collins, 1995) 384.

7. Eisler, *Sacred Pleasure*, 385.

8. Maria Shriver, "A Woman's Nation Changes Everything," in Heather Boushey and Ann O'Leary, Eds., *The Shriver Report -- A Woman's Nation Changes Everything* (Washington, DC: A Study by Maria Shriver and the Center for American Progress, 2009) 8.

9. Shriver, "A Woman's Nation Changes Everything," *The Shriver Report*, 11.

10. Michael Kimmel, "Has a Man's World Become a Woman's Nation?" in Heather Boushey and Ann O'Leary, Eds.,*The Shriver Report—A Woman's Nation Changes Everything* (Washington, DC: A Study by Maria Shriver and the Center for American Progress, 2009), 324.

11. Kimmel, "Has a Man's World Become a Woman's Nation?" *The Shriver Report*, 354.

12. Kimmel, "Has a Man's World Become a Woman's Nation?" *The Shriver Report*, 344.

13. Kimmel, "Has a Man's World Become a Woman's Nation?" *The Shriver Report*, 345.

14. Rosalind Barnett and Caryl Rivers, *She Works/He Works*, (Cambridge, MA: Harvard University Press, 1996) 3.

15. Barnett and Rivers, *She Works/He Works*, 1.

16. Julia Baird, "Beyond the Bad Boys," *Newsweek,* April 19, 2010.

17. Stephanie Coontz, "Sharing the Load," in Heather Boushey and Ann O'Leary, Eds., *The Shriver Report—A Woman's Nation Changes Everything* (Washington DC: A Study by Maria Shriver and the Center for American Progress, 2009) 372.
18. Coontz, "Sharing the Load," *The Shriver Report*, 376.
19. Coontz, "Sharing the Load," *The Shriver Report*, 377.
20. Cowdery and Knudson-Martin, "The Construction of Motherhood: Tasks, Relational Connection, and Gender Equality, *Family Relations,* 54 (July 2005), 335-345.
21. Brian Braiker, "Just Don't Call Me Mr. Mom," *Newsweek*, October 8, 2007.
22. Braiker, "Just Don't Call Me Mr. Mom," *Newsweek.*
23. Kimmel, "Has a Man's World Become a Woman's Nation," *The Shriver Report*, 352.
24. Kimmel, "Has a Man's World Become a Woman's Nation," *The Shriver Report*, 353. Note: Kimmel points out that the latter may be caused, at least in part, by a change of attitude on the part of wives and female partners who, when their husbands or male partners help them with the housework and childcare, suffer less resentment and stress than if they have had to assume responsibility for domestic chores by themselves.
25. Kimmel, "Has a Man's World Become a Woman's Nation," *The Shriver Report*, 353.
26. Eisler, *Sacred Pleasure*, 65.
27. Marie C. Wilson, *Closing the Leadership Gap: Why Women Can and Must Help Run the World*, (London: Penguin Books, Ltd., 2004) 7.
28. Wilson, *Closing the Leadership Gap*, 8.

29. King, *Creating Partnerships*, 100.
30. King, *Creating Partnerships*, 49.
31. King, *Creating Partnerships*, 80.
32. Daniel Goleman, *Emotional Intelligence*, (New York: Bantam Books, 1997) 153.
33. Goleman, *Emotional Intelligence,* 153.
34. Daniel Goleman "What Makes a Leader?" *Harvard Business Review,* Nov.-Dec. 1998.
35. Goleman, "What Makes a Leader?" *Harvard Business Review*
36. Chip R. Bell and Oren Harari, "The New (beep, beep) Rules of HRD," *Training and Development*, No. 54, Aug. 2000 p. 45.
37. Tony Dokoupil and Andrew Romano, "Men's Lib," *Newsweek*, September 27, 2010.
38. Dokoupil and Romano, "Men's Lib, *Newsweek*.
39. Coontz, "Sharing the Load," *The Shriver Report*, 377.
40. Courtney E. Martin, "Transcending 9 to 5," in Heather Boushey and Ann O'Leary, Eds., *The Shriver Report --A Woman's Nation Changes Everything* (Washington, DC: A Study by Maria Shriver and the Center for American Progress, 2009) 388.
41. Anna Quindlen, "The End of Swagger," *Newsweek,* Feb. 9, 2009.
42. Wilson, *Closing the Leadership Gap*, 11.
43. Ann Crittenden, *The Price of Motherhood,* (New York: Henry Holt and Company, LLC, 2001) 249.
44. Greg Mortenson and David Oliver Relin *Three Cups of Tea* (New York: Penguin Books, 2006) 234.
45. "A Short History of Grameen Bank," *Bank for the Poor: Grameen Bank.*, http://grameen-info.org.

46. Kim Azzarelli and Melanne Verveer, "Hiring the Third Billion," *Newsweek*, February 6, 2012.

47. Eisler, *Sacred Pleasure,* 343.

48. Crittenden*, The Price of Motherhood,* 248.

49. Dokoupil, and Romano, "Men's Lib," *Newsweek.*

50. Riane Eisler, *The Power of Partnership,* (Novato, CA: New World Library, 2002) 195.

51. Eisler, *The Power of Partnership*, 188.

52. Gloria Steinem, *Revolution From Within* (Boston, MA: Little Brown and Company, 1992) 268.

53. Barry K. Weinhold and Janae B. Weinhold, *Breaking Free of the Codependency Trap,* (New York: MJF Books, 1989) 220.

54. Johnson, *The Gender Knot*, 240.

55. Johnson, *The Gender Knot*, 165.

Afterward

1.   Andrew Das,"U.S. Soccer and Women's Players Agree to Settle Equal Pay Lawsuit,", *The N.Y. Times, Digital*, https://www.nytimes.com/2022/02/22/sports/soccer/us-womens-soccer-equal-pay.html

2.   Robert Klemko,"A Police Chief is hiring female officers to fix 'toxic' policing in Omaha, Nebraska" *Washington Post, Digita*l, March 26, 2022.

3.   Naomi Moriyama and William Doyle, "This is what a country run by women looks like," *CNN Digital,* March 8, 2022.

4.   https://borgenprojectorg/womens-rights-in-iceland/

5.   https://www.freepressunlimited.org/en/current/eu-call-justice-maria-ressa?

6.   Liz Plank, *For the Love of Men: A New Vision for Mindful Masculinity,* (New York, NY: St. Martins Press) 76.

7. Plank, *For the Love of Men: A New Vision for Mindful Masculinity*, 78.

8. Plank, *For the Love of Men: A New Vision for Mindful Masculinity*, 94.

9. Courtney Kube, "Starting Tuesday, al U. S. military veterans in suicidal crisis will be eligible for free care at any VA or Private Facility," *NBC News Digital*, January 13, 2023.

10. Jose A Del Real, "The Re-invention of a Real Man," *Washington Post Digital*, May 23, 2022.

11. Plank, *For the Love of Men: A New Vision for Mindful Masculinity*, 290.

12. Plank, *For the Love of Men: A New Vision for Mindful Masculinity*, 292.

13. Plank, *For the Love of Men: A New Vision for Mindful Masculinity*, 294.